Ghost Habits

How To Do Something
When You Can't Do Anything

N.D. Olson

HALVEN

Ghost Habits: How To Do Something When You Can't Do Anything

Published by Halven Media

ISBN: 978-91-989099-0-6 (Paperback)
ISBN: 978-91-989099-1-3 (eBook)

Book Cover by Geoffrey Bunting

To O, *in all the world there was only you*

To K, *from the morning I met you,*
life has been a million times lovelier

Contents

Introduction

Everything You've Tried So Far Has Failed You

Let's be real.

You're not gonna follow the expert advice on how to focus and get things done. You won't wake up at 5:30 a.m. every morning, yawn and stretch as the birds cheerfully chirp outside your window, with the warm sunlight streaming into your bedroom, then sit down at the kitchen table with your mug of hot chai latte and rainbow glitter pens to journal about all the wonderful things you're going to do that day.

We both know that's not going to happen. Maybe you can muster the energy to do it for a few days or a week, but it won't become your thing.

Neither will you make extensive daily to-do lists, track how many glasses of water you drank, how many loads of laundry you folded, or how many meetings you attended, and check each one off on your nifty little phone app throughout the day.

It ain't gonna happen.

Because if you could do it and wanted to do it, you wouldn't, at this very moment, be looking for information about how to do it. That's just who you are. That's the standard advice we're told to follow. It seems helpful, but it's unrealistic.

You're not lazy because you can't follow the strategies they throw at you. You're anything but. You put a lot of effort into your tasks and chores, but they don't help you make the most of your time or get them done. You only feel bad about yourself.

Many of those struggling with these problems are at the opposite end of the financial and class spectrum. If anything, we're mired in credit card or student loan debt and possibly have a negative net worth well beyond our thirties or forties. We might be grappling with expensive healthcare bills. Some of us have learned the hard truth that poverty (and lower-middle-class life) is expensive. We've been nickel and dimed all our lives and learned to expect it.

For some of us, it's even harder than it looks from the outside. Chronic pain, fatigue conditions, and other physical problems are more common in neurodivergent people than most think, and they stack on top of everything else you're carrying. When it's like that, getting through it is all you can do. There's nothing more to give. These steps don't expect you to start where everyone else does.

You feel inadequate when you're putting maximum energy into bettering your life and achieving your goals. You consider it a failure on your part, which makes it all the more difficult to gather the motivation to pick yourself up and try again.

We feel bad because we realize what helps others doesn't help us. Why would it? We're all wildly different people from different backgrounds and situations. There is no One-Size-Fits-All approach. What helps one person won't help the next. When we accept those differences, we can stop fighting the wrong approach.

It's not habits, routines, emotions, energy levels, focus, or any other single cause. Multiple factors go into taking you from an initial task to a completed task. Changing only one or two things won't get the results you desire.

If you're looking to finish chores around your house, make your work responsibilities easier, start your own business, find your dream job, or do anything else you want but can't, you can achieve it. It just takes a different approach.

This book is that different approach. It's habit-free, routine-free, and discipline-free. That goes squarely against the popular advice, but if habits, routines, and discipline don't work for you, as they don't for many of us, there is another way.

What to Expect

You're going to stop using the **Ghost Habits**.

Not today and maybe not this week, but eventually you'll abandon them.

Most productivity books assume you'll use their advice forever and ever. Morning routines, daily habits, weekly reviews. When you stop, you've failed.

Ghost Habits assumes you'll **crash** and burn out. You'll get sick, busy, or overwhelmed, and eventually you'll stop.

Later in this book, you'll learn how to restart. One sheet of paper with four boxes is your way back in. You'll restart when you're ready.

If you're expecting something that turns you into a productivity machine who never stumbles, wrong book. If you're expecting something that acknowledges you're going to stumble and shows you how to get back up, keep reading.

A Quick Note About Habits

Some people use habits to be productive. I don't.

If you have a morning routine that works or habit tracking that motivates you, keep doing it. There are good books about building neurodivergent-friendly habits. This isn't one of them.

Most productivity advice assumes habits are the foundation. Wake up at the same time every day, do your morning routine, track your streaks, and build consistency. If you can do that and it helps, great. Go for it.

But if you've tried building habits multiple times and they don't stick, you don't need to keep trying. You can skip that entire approach and still get things done. That's not a Plan B because you failed at the real way. It's a completely different way.

Throughout this book, I'll give you strategies and tools. If any of them drain your energy, stop using them. This should be easier than what you were doing before. If it's not, you're either overcomplicating it or that particular tool isn't right for you right now.

Why I Call Them Ghost Habits

The name works two ways. These are tools that appear when you need them and disappear when you don't, like ghosts that show up and vanish on their own schedule. But you're also doing the ghosting. The habits, routines, and systems that were never built for how you function? Ghost them. Walk away without explaining yourself. You don't owe productivity culture a breakup conversation.

What's left after you've ghosted all of that is what's going to help you get things done. That's what this book is.

The Object at Rest Problem

There's a reason we start with the smallest possible thing and build from there.

When you're paralyzed and can't do anything, you're stuck. There's a name for it, **ADHD inertia**, and it works exactly like it sounds. The longer nothing happens, the harder it becomes to start. But the opposite is also true. Once you're moving, even a little, it becomes easier to keep going, getting a snack, making coffee, writing one email, and washing the dishes. Each small action makes the next one easier than the last.

This is why you don't start with your hardest task. You start with the easiest possible thing to get things rolling. Once you're in motion, you might find yourself doing things you couldn't have started from a standstill. Sometimes that momentum carries you through the whole day. Sometimes it carries you through one more task and then you're done. Either way, you did something.

That's not always how it goes, though. Sometimes you're already fired up and want to go straight at the big thing. Ghost Habit #5 covers that.

The **Six Survival Steps** get you through the days when doing something feels impossible. The eight Ghost Habits keep you functioning on the other days. The rest of this book shows you how to use what you can do so you're paralyzed less often.

How to Use This Book

You can read this book in order from start to finish, or you can skip around to the chapters that feel most relevant right now. Each chapter builds on the previous ones and is also designed to stand alone. If you need help with a problem, jump straight to that chapter. Need to figure out which task to do? Go to Ghost Habit #4. Can't focus? Go to Ghost Habit #7. Completely paralyzed? The Six Survival Steps coming up next are for exactly that moment.

This book focuses on what you can do, whether or not medication is part of your life.

The eight Ghost Habits don't have to be implemented in order. You don't have to use all of them. Start with whichever one feels easiest or most helpful. Add more as you need them. Drop the ones that don't work for you.

Most books give you homework at the end of every chapter. You already have enough to do. Each chapter ends with a Quick Take, a summary of the key points.

The Six Survival Steps

What Do You Do When You Can't Do Anything?

That's the real question. Not "how do I be more productive next week" or "how do I build better habits." The question is, what do I do in this moment, when I'm staring at my to-do list, and I can't make myself do a single thing on it?

You know the feeling. You're completely stuck. You need to do something, anything, but your brain won't cooperate. The dishes are piling up, the emails are piling up, the deadlines are piling up, and you're sitting there doing absolutely nothing. Or worse, you're doing something you don't even enjoy because at least it's not that thing you're supposed to be doing.

People tell you to "just do it." Great advice. But completely useless when you're in full lockdown mode.

Before the steps: The survival check.

Your brain is going to tell you what feels urgent, but it's probably lying. Before anything else, check if there's something that will cause actual harm or immediate serious **consequences** if not done in the next few hours.

Medication you take on a schedule, feeding a pet or person who depends on you, eating something if you haven't eaten today, or drinking water if you're dehydrated. Showing up to something you absolutely cannot miss, like a work shift, picking up your kid, or a critical appointment. This means anything medical or time-sensitive.

That's the list. Not showering, cleaning, or sending emails, and not paying bills unless your power is being shut off today. Nothing that feels pressing but won't hurt you if it waits.

Can you do these? If you can't, you need help from another person. Call or text someone. If you can, take care of that first and then come back to Step 1. If you don't have anything time-sensitive, keep reading.

Step 1: Accept that you can't do anything else right now.

If you can't do anything, stop beating yourself up about it. Stop trying to force yourself into doing the thing you're supposed to do. It hasn't worked for the last hour, and it won't work for the next hour.

Step 2: Ask yourself if you can do something.

Can you sit up? Can you move to a different spot? Can you get a glass of water? Can you pet the cat?

If the answer is no, if you're truly unable to do even that, then you need rest. Take a nap. Close your eyes and take a break. You're depleted, and rest is the only thing that will help.

But if the answer is yes, then you have a place to start.

Step 3: Do the smallest possible thing.

Skip the list entirely. Try to do the smallest thing you can physically make yourself do in this moment. Eat something. Open a window. Play music. Whatever you can do.

Why? You think you can't do anything. You need to prove that you're wrong, even if it's something minor. You're trying to break the paralysis here.

Step 4: Once you've done that one small thing, ask yourself if you can do one more.

If you can't, stop. You've done something. But if you can, if you have a tiny bit of momentum, do one more small thing, still off the list. Make yourself a cup of tea. Fold a blanket. Brush your teeth. Empty the trash bin. You're picking up speed.

Step 5: Check if there's anything you need to do today to keep your life from falling apart.

You've already taken care of the survival needs and done something to get moving. What has to happen today? Do you need to be somewhere? Do you need to respond to one important email? If yes, can you do the absolute minimum? You're trying to get through the day without making things worse.

Step 6: If you have any energy left, look at your tasks and see if there's anything you feel like doing.

You've done more than you thought you could. Use what's left on whatever you can, even if it's minor and doesn't have to be done today.

This is how you do something when you can't do anything. The smallest possible thing, then maybe one more, then maybe one more after that.

Some days, "something" is a full day's work. Other days, it's eating a meal and taking a shower. You gave it everything you could.

The Struggle Is Real

This Is for You

There is an entire group of people out there like me who are searching for ways to do more with their lives. We feel alone. We can't talk about it because no one understands. If you're reading this, you're probably one of them. People think your condition is an excuse not to do what's expected of everyone else, or they think you're faking it altogether.

We can't see an end to it. The system isn't made for us. You might have ADHD, autism, dyslexia, OCD, bipolar disorder, PTSD, anxiety, depression, brain injury, chronic migraines, or a combination of these. Whether you have a diagnosis or simply believe you have one of these conditions, you know the struggle to wake up every day and try to be your best in a world where the rules don't work for you.

It's a world you don't understand, and that doesn't understand you. Our conditions manifest differently in us, but we share some commonalities. At the very least, they draw us away from our tasks toward unproductive and sometimes unhealthy places.

We're constantly told we're not doing enough to succeed. That plays like a broken record when we spend every day striving to get our lives in a better place. We already know what it's like to be told we're not good enough or working hard enough. Some of us are even struggling to access the most basic necessities of life, like food and housing.

So, let me ask you, have you tried to do anything at all in your life? Believe me, I know the answer. I've heard it a million times.

I've Been There

I've spent years researching this. Every format I could find, lectures, articles, courses, and conversations with people who live it every day. Years of testing it on myself and helping others do the same.

As a neurodivergent person myself, I know how hard it is to get people to understand the monumental effort you make. In their eyes, you haven't done anything because they don't see the grand results they expect.

My efforts to track my expenses or start a new business failed because I couldn't get started, couldn't decide what to do first, or couldn't focus long enough to complete it. But that doesn't mean I didn't give it my maximum attention and effort.

There may have been a time when you were better able to function, but a life event, chronic illness, physical disability, a painful breakup, a move away from loved ones, or a loss has set you back, and you're struggling to keep your head above water.

Life isn't a cakewalk for anyone in our neurodiverse world, though the **neurotypicals** tend to fit better within society as it is. They find it easier to excel in the classroom, office life, and daily social interactions. You might not always read the room. Like telling a coworker that honey is bee vomit when they didn't ask. And then diving in to explain the full process.

Because you don't intuitively know how to do it, you'll have more difficulty completing even the simplest tasks. It's not that you can't eventually do them, but you'll need to work longer and more strategically to do so.

Most of your attempts at building a normal life fall short. You may jump from job to job, always believing this will be the one for you, but after a short time, you send off your resignation email or stop showing up altogether. You might **mask** your condition long enough to get hired, but soon it comes off, and it all goes downhill.

Your skills don't translate well in our day-to-day world, impairing your ability to complete basic tasks, let alone climb the ladder to a high-paying career.

At home, you can't keep up with the household chores. Maybe you're living in a sparsely furnished space with less to clean. Or you live in a cluttered home because you soothe yourself with your much-loved possessions.

You may not see where you're going wrong or how to fix it. Or you see the problem but can't fix it. This can cause your anxiety to skyrocket or send you into a tailspin of depression, compounding the situation even more.

Some of you are reading this from a place where the basics aren't covered. Not "I should put 10% more into my 401(k)" basics. Rent. Food. Whether the electricity gets shut off. The productivity advice that tells you to optimize your mornings and outsource your laundry wasn't written with you in mind, and you could see that before you finished the first page.

This book doesn't fix any of that. What it can do is work from wherever you are, even when you feel you're at the bottom. The tools in here don't require a gym membership or a therapist or a morning that's within your control. They were built for people whose margin is always thin, because that's how most of us live.

People struggling with neurodivergent conditions are not a special group. Current studies estimate that as many as 20% of the global population have at least one neurodivergent condition. Take a look around your classroom, workplace, or community.

That's a sizable percentage of humanity struggling with productivity and life in general.

Many of us never got help. Our parents didn't know, our teachers didn't recognize it, and our doctors missed it. The academic programs, accommodations, therapy, and training that could have helped were either unavailable, unaffordable, or no one thought to point us toward them. That meant struggling a little harder for some people. For others, it meant decades of damage that didn't have to happen.

Some neurodivergent people find niches where their wiring is an advantage. With the right field, a favorable environment, and enough flexibility to function, they can do well. But it's not the norm, and pretending otherwise doesn't help the people who haven't found it yet.

For most of us, the workplace was built for someone else, and we're just trying to survive in it.

That's a lot working against you.

We block out the hustle bros and productivity gurus who assure us that all our problems stem from laziness and lack of habits and routines. We can identify the pieces that fit our abilities and assemble them in a way that makes sense for us.

Staying One Step Ahead of Disaster

There was a time in my life when my lack of executive function paralyzed me. Most people can't understand what that means because they've never experienced it to a critical extent. From waking up until falling asleep, I did nothing constructive.

The hours slipped away. I couldn't manage my time to do the things I wanted to do, either at home or at work. Unable to prioritize the tasks I needed to do, I did only what was necessary to get through another day.

Whether it was going to a job I hated and watching each second tick by on the clock, or making the least possible effort to clean, run errands, and keep food in the cabinets, it was almost too much for me. At that time, getting kicked out on the street was a worse alternative, so I did just enough to stay housed and fed.

On rare days, I'd be inspired to improve my situation once and for all, yet I struggled with nearly every task I faced. I'd try the latest productivity strategy to get my life in order and give it up after a few days. Nothing worked for me. Procrastination was king. I put everything off until tomorrow.

I didn't care about exercising or maintaining a healthy diet. I had all the time in the world in the future. I'd get around to it later, I told myself.

But one day, the scales tipped, literally. I stepped on my digital scale and realized my perfectly ripped physique from years of cycling was gone, obscured by half a decade of fast food and daily screen time. Even worse, I lost sight of 30, and 40 seemed closer than ever.

While the "ripped" part may be slightly exaggerated, that moment was a massive wake-up call. I needed to get my life back in order and figure out how to do the things I'd been avoiding.

It isn't that if you do A, B, and C, then naturally D, E, and F will fall into place. We don't live in Magic Pony Land, where everything is rainbows and butterflies, and it all comes to a satisfyingly sweet, happy ending.

My situation may sound extreme, but it's not uncommon. Life for people like me is a constant battle of weighing our options, choosing the least challenging necessary tasks, and putting in the minimum effort to complete them. Like pulling an all-nighter to cram for an exam, you try to stay one step above the worst possible option at every moment.

But when the downside outweighs the upside, that's when we finally get moving.

Dude, Where's My Focus?

You say you can't do anything, but some activities take up your time every day, right? Even if it's only playing video games, scrolling through social media, watching Netflix, or spending all day at your boring day job, before going home and crashing in your bed for 10 hours.

We want to believe other people can do it for us and that they have the perfect solutions we're so desperately searching for. If we follow their script to a T, magic will happen. We'll get the fixes we need and the life we dream of. We know it's probably too good to be true, but we cling to that belief anyway.

Sometimes we don't even know what we're searching for, but when we believe that someone is handing us the ultimate cheat code that solves our problems, we tend to listen. It's easy to accept almost any solution when we feel lost. It's the relief we seek to take the weight off our tired, anxious brains. Then we throw ourselves into it. When it doesn't help, we're right back where we started. Only this time, we're more exhausted, frustrated, and further behind.

If you're a woodworker trying to build a desk, you don't follow instructions to bake a cake. They're perfect for baking, useless for furniture. So why do we think instructions that work for neurotypical people will work for us?

Welcome to the Underachievers Club

Unfortunately, neurodivergent people face staggering odds when it comes to finding a suitable career and staying employed in it. Unemployment among neurodivergent adults is significantly higher than in the general population, and for adults with autism, the number may reach upwards of 85%.

Our skills generally don't transfer to full-time employment as well as those of neurotypical employees.

A lot of that energy gets spent before the day even starts. We make an enormous effort at work, school, and in public, appearing to function normally. Suppressing our **stims**, forcing eye contact, acting out all the social scripts that come naturally to others, while staying quiet about how overwhelmed we are. That's what people call masking. By the time we get home, the energy that was supposed to go toward our own lives is already long gone. We pay that cost every day.

We can't take any old job. If it doesn't fit our requirements, it probably won't lead to lasting employment. Many of us living outside urban areas have limited job prospects and sparse or nonexistent public transportation if we can't drive ourselves. All of that drastically limits our ability to support ourselves through traditional employment.

Neurodivergence itself is a spectrum. Some can work the same job every day for 40 years. At the other end of the spectrum, you may never hold a job at all. Someone who received assistance and had parents who gave them a good start can't understand how someone thrown out of the house at 18 has struggled to make their way in life. But that's no different from the neurotypical world. We don't realize the enormity of other people's struggles because we experience life differently.

Some of us are fortunate enough to find niches in fields like academia, tech, entrepreneurship, or a family-owned business, where, despite our continued struggles, we can comfortably support ourselves.

Still, others haven't done things society labels as successful, especially in our professional lives. It's not that we don't have the potential, but that we lack the organizational skills and follow-through to reach it. We can be sensitive to work environments, have limited social skills, and struggle with job interviews. We may only have the strength to work a 4-hour day or three days a week.

Those things, saddled with whatever other conditions we have, consistently hold us back from achieving what we want in life and staying gainfully employed.

You may have an invisible or physical disability you didn't ask for. Yet it is the people who don't have it, or who have minimal hardships, who strut around crowing that they have jobs and houses and good lives and contribute to the world as productive members of society, making you believe you need to "get over it" and do it, too.

People think it's mostly by choice that we don't overcome our circumstances. We are the ones society looks down on. In their eyes, you came from a disadvantaged background, you have a mental condition, you're less than, you're broken. They look at us with pity and occasionally outright hostility.

We don't all embrace the idea that 24/7 hard work should be the most essential tenet in life. They feel sorry for you but still think you're lazy. You didn't try hard enough to overcome every obstacle thrown at you.

Productivity advice was built for a specific kind of person. Neurotypical, sure. But also a specific class of person.

It makes self-help experts and productivity gurus a lot of money. It's tailor-made for people who want to be part of hustle culture or believe they should be, but it's not for everyone. Few of the expert suggestions are helpful in practical terms for those who feel outside the norm.

Multimillionaire and billionaire CEOs, tech rock stars, celebrities, and self-proclaimed thought leaders don't have much practical advice to apply directly to your life. But their books are filled with gushing forewords, over-the-top endorsements from celebrity friends, and page after page touting their credentials, volunteer work, and charitable donations to make themselves look good. All of it designed to push their brands.

That escapism is exciting for us to daydream about. Most of us in the working class are merely trying to survive.

Many of these productivity gurus who made their fortunes in the corporate world now proclaim to have all the answers on how to fix you. They sell you expensive guides and masterclasses meant to reinforce a single idea. If we could stop being lazy, we could be as ultra-productive and well-off as they are.

But, unlike them, we never had the luxury of building our fortunes in the corporate world or the fallback of returning to it if real life didn't work out. That's the world most of us are working in. This book is built for that world, not the one they're selling.

I didn't manage to *Forrest Gump* my way through life. I haven't happily fallen into circumstances that, unbeknownst to me, would change my life for the better.

There's nothing wrong with deciding you don't want to be part of the current hustle culture. Every generation has had people who don't fit the hustle culture mold. That's not new. What's new is understanding why. We can carve out a niche for ourselves, play by our own rules, and do what we can to build a fulfilling life. It's been done for decades. Unfortunately, we don't always have the tools to do that because we've been conditioned to believe the conventional way is the only way.

Years ago, I decided it was time to put it down on paper, initially out of a strong sense of resentment. I was tired of hearing that I was lazy, which was why I never became "somebody." I didn't understand how I had all but squandered my youthful potential. I struggled from childhood through nearly middle adulthood before I finally started looking into why none of it worked for me. I still looked like a lazy slacker.

I'm not exceptional, but I've learned that I'm not the audience most of the leading productivity advice is aimed at.

You're different. Just like everyone else.

Welcome to the Club.

Getting Here Was the Hard Part

If you've reached 40, 50, 60, 70+ years old and are still struggling with the most basic areas of your life, you're a survivor. You probably lived through some dark times and learned most of your lessons the hard way. If you're younger, congratulations on realizing you need to discover your way before you've gone too far down the wrong road.

Consider yourself fortunate if you received a diagnosis and support as a child. Many of us missed that boat completely.

Some of you are reading this with a diagnosis you got last year, or last month, and a lifetime of experiences that suddenly make sense. That recalibration takes time. It doesn't hand you the answers, though, because knowing why doesn't automatically fix anything. It only changes what you understand about your life.

Others have been told their whole lives to get over it, try harder, and stop making excuses. By people who should have known better and by people who truly didn't understand. Either way, the dismissal does damage. Both leave you trying to function without the tools or the support you needed, figuring it out alone. If that's your history, this book isn't going to tell you to get over anything.

As you grow older, receiving support as a neurodivergent adult becomes much more complicated. There is no magic fix.

When you were younger, there was at least structure around you. You had school, someone else's schedule to follow, teachers who noticed when something was wrong, even if they didn't know what to do about it. That disappears as you get older. Adult life hands you a wide-open field and tells you to build your own structure from scratch, which is exactly the thing you struggle to do most.

Your responsibilities compound, too. You're juggling more than just getting yourself through the day anymore. There are bills, jobs, relationships, possibly kids or aging parents, in a world that assumes you have everything running smoothly because you're a grown adult. The divide between what's expected of you and what you can manage gets wider.

And then there's the cost of decades of hiding it. You've spent years writing scripts for every occasion and performing them on demand. By the time you're in your thirties or forties or beyond, you've been paying the price for that for a long time.

Whether your symptoms have worsened or life has gotten harder, the career struggle is the same.

It's a fairly common, yet unfortunate, belief that your level of intelligence somehow equates to financial success, but if you're struggling with severe **executive dysfunction**, you'll be lucky to find your career at all. You may excel at some tasks but be woefully deficient in others. How can you succeed in a job with a skill set like that when you're expected to be a superhuman jack-of-all-trades for your employers? They're searching for that puzzle piece that fits their needs, but you're never the right fit. Or, more frustratingly, you're almost the right fit, just a little off. But that's not good enough. It won't lead to that job or the assignment.

I always heard that success meant going to a top university for a tech or business degree, getting a comfortable 9-to-5, a signing bonus, stock options, and retiring early with a hefty 401(k). That was the formula. Artists, service workers, English majors, anyone not in the right career? They just hadn't tried hard enough.

Nobody told us the formula had different requirements buried in the fine print.

This advice assumes you can work full-time while in school. That you can network your way into jobs when social interaction exhausts you. That you have the executive function to navigate corporate hierarchies. That you can maintain the consistency these paths require.

I finally got tired of it and decided that if I can't fit into that world, I'll build my own path. At some point, you stop trying to fix yourself and start figuring out what helps you.

Why You Can't Get Started (And Why That's Not Your Fault)

The Chaos in Your Brain

On my worst days, I felt I could never make a decent effort. We've all been there. How do you focus when your mind is constantly scattered? You can't concentrate on a single thought because your mind is everywhere, contemplating everything you see, past negative thoughts and memories, and what might be lurking around the next corner. You are an expert at overthinking every situation, replaying past conversations in your head, and analyzing the words you said or should have said. It's utterly exhausting.

At its extreme, the thoughts are like a 50-lane freeway that merges into a single lane. To say it's a traffic jam is an understatement. Nothing gets through because it's a jumble of cars blocking all the lanes. None of the cars will yield to the others. They're all vying for attention, their drivers screaming, honking, and revving their engines in a constant fit of road rage. It's impossible to focus on a single thought.

Or on the flip side, maybe you've given up? Your mind is now like a dark, empty void. You want to do things, but you've convinced yourself that it's a lost cause. Why bother? Nothing has helped you in the past. Your luck won't change now.

Whatever circumstances brought you to this place in your life, you can get out.

I've Tried Everything

I've tried to do things outside my abilities for most of my life. Filled out the 200-question personality quizzes, journaled my emotions, and tried to follow the popular advice meticulously. None of it helped. I kept doing the same things, expecting something to change, but it never did. This book is built on accepting that I will never fit the mold of someone who can do those things.

Experts in organization and time management, all the people who claim to do what we can't, offer tons of tips on how to deal with this. No matter how many tips they offer, my brain won't respond to them any differently.

I won't tell you it's painless. You'll have setbacks. You'll be disappointed in yourself. You're already dealing with enough, and this adds to it.

As unfair as it is, you may need to make ten times the effort to get the same results as others. That's daily life for most of us.

The rest of this book is written for how you think.

The Many Faces of Paralysis

Paralysis isn't one thing. These are the ones that come up most often for many neurodivergent people and the ones this book has tools for.

Decision paralysis hits when you have too many options. You've got 25 things on your list, and you lock up when you try to choose one. So you do nothing, or you switch between tasks every five minutes, never finishing any of them.

Anticipation paralysis happens before you even start. You're dreading the task so much that you can't make yourself begin. Once you're doing it, it's fine. Getting there is the problem. You'll do anything else, even tasks you normally hate, to avoid that first move.

Perfectionism paralysis keeps you frozen because you're terrified of doing it wrong. If you can't do it perfectly, you won't do it at all. The project sits there haunting you as you research and prepare, but you never start.

Overwhelm paralysis strikes when the task feels too big. You don't know where to start, so you don't.

You can't even break it into smaller pieces because even that feels like too much work.

Known task paralysis is when you already know exactly how something goes before you start, and that's why you can't begin it. You've done this before and you've already decided you don't want to do it. You can't make yourself begin something you already know everything about, like dropping off a package that's been sitting by the door for two weeks before the return window closes, or throwing out all the expired food in your fridge or pantry.

Demand paralysis hits when someone else puts a clock on you. Your boss needs something in fifteen minutes. Your teacher announced an in-class essay. Someone is standing there waiting for an answer right now. For a lot of us, that kind of external pressure shuts us down completely. The more pressure they apply, the harder it gets. The task you could do fine on your own becomes impossible the moment someone else puts a demand on you.

All of these are common in neurodivergent people, and recognizing which type you're dealing with helps you pick the right tool.

The Dopamine Loop

You need to understand why you function the way you do. Why habits don't stick. Why motivation disappears. Why you can focus for hours on a video game but can't make yourself reply to one text message.

The answer for most of us is **dopamine**.

Say what you want about caffeine or even sugar, but you're probably more driven by dopamine than you realize.

Dopamine is a chemical neurotransmitter produced in the brain that signals potential rewards. Dopamine fires for anything that looks like it might feel good or be more fun than the boring tasks you have to do, which is why getting that next dopamine hit is as easy as looking at your phone. We crave it constantly.

The reward is not without its cost. Once something becomes routine and predictable, the signal gets weaker. But we still want it. That's why a new game holds your attention for hours, and the game you couldn't stop playing last month is forgotten. That's also exactly why habits stop working. The novelty wears off, the dopamine disappears, and so does the motivation.

For some people, the seeking never stops. What starts as reaching for the phone instead of work can escalate into patterns that are truly hard to break. Less productivity, failing careers, and, in serious cases, self-destructive behaviors like alcohol and drugs.

Neurotypical productivity advice is built for neurotypical dopamine. That's not you.

The Thing You Do Instead

We tend to seek **anti-tasks** as alternatives to the things we don't want to do. I call them anti-tasks rather than distractions because distraction implies something happening to you. An anti-task is something you actively choose because it meets a need your real task doesn't.

Scrolling TikTok when you should be writing. Playing games when you should be studying. Organizing your bookshelf when you should be making that phone call. Cleaning the kitchen when you should be answering an email.

You've been told these are distractions, procrastination, and laziness, but they're not.

You're chasing dopamine, rest, escape, or novelty, and when your real task doesn't provide what you need right now, you find something that does.

When the task is too boring, you seek dopamine elsewhere, and you end up **doomscrolling** social media for an hour.

When the task makes you anxious, you're looking for an escape, and suddenly you're pacing and reorganizing your kitchen.

When you're exhausted, you seek rest and binge-watch 16 episodes of *Parks and Rec* instead.

Anti-tasks aren't random distractions that happen to you. They're your solution to a problem with your current task, which means they're giving you information about what you need.

The Five Types of Anti-Tasks

Anti-tasks fall into five categories based on what need you're trying to meet.

Dopamine-seeking anti-tasks are the ones people think about when they talk about procrastination. Social media, games, shopping, and anything that gives quick hits of pleasure. At one time, I was ordering everything online, and it wasn't only because the last thing I wanted to do was face people in public. I'd spend hours combing the internet to find a certain pair of shoes at a rock-bottom price, and when I hit that Buy button, it felt good. You go for these when your task is tedious or unrewarding, and you need something that feels good right this minute.

Rest-seeking anti-tasks are low-effort activities like scrolling through your phone, watching TV, or lying on the couch. They aren't restful in the same way that sleep is restful, but they feel easier than the task you're avoiding. You sit down to start your work and take a minute to collect your thoughts before you begin, and before you know it, you've been watching cat videos for 45 minutes.

You'll never catch me willingly scrubbing the kitchen floor, but if I have to make a phone call that's making me anxious, I'll do anything to put it off and not think about it. That's an **escape-seeking anti-task**. Cleaning, organizing, busywork, and other productive-looking activities that aren't the thing you're supposed to do. The real task creates anxiety, and doing something else that seems productive makes you feel better about avoiding it.

Novelty-seeking anti-tasks appear when your current task has become dull or repetitive, and you need something interesting to think about instead. You're hard at work writing your paper for your Economics class when you look up a fact on Wikipedia, and soon you're down the rabbit hole reading about The Great Emu War of 1932. New projects, ideas, and research completely unrelated to what you're supposed to be doing are the novelty-seeking anti-task.

Social anti-tasks are about connection. Sometimes you need to know someone else is there before you can focus again. Texting, checking email, calling someone, or hanging around the coffee machine because you'll always find a chat there. You want these when you're feeling isolated or when you're afraid you're missing something while you're stuck doing your task alone. It's times like these when I remember I need to reply to the last text my BFF sent a week ago.

Recognize the Pattern

Try this for one week. Whenever you go for an anti-task, pay attention to what the real task was, what anti-task you chose instead, what time of day it happened, and how you were feeling when you dropped your real task.

Were you bored, anxious, tired, restless, or something else?

The patterns should become apparent pretty quickly. You might go for social anti-tasks like texting a friend when you're anxious and you need connection, dopamine anti-tasks like online shopping when you're bored, and escape anti-tasks like rearranging your sock drawer when you're overwhelmed. In all of these, your brain is finding a way to feel like it's doing something.

Outsmart Your Anti-tasks

When you sit down to work and you immediately want to do anything else, you're facing your anti-tasks. You can't eliminate them by deleting apps or blocking websites because those don't delete the need you're trying to meet.

Start by recognizing when you're choosing an anti-task. You reach for your phone, open yet another browser tab, or suddenly remember you need to alphabetize your Pop figure collection again. You're looking for an escape route.

Ask yourself what the anti-task is telling you it needs.

When it's clear you know what you need, you can either address that need differently or recognize you might need to do the anti-task right now.

If you need dopamine, build a small reward into your task. Finish one section and get a snack. Complete the email and check one social media app. If you're like me and rewards aren't for you, listen to music or a podcast to get the boost you need to finish the task.

Do a smaller version of the task if you need escape because the task makes you anxious. Can't write the whole report? Write the outline. Unable to make a phone call? Write down what you're going to say first in your Notes app. Rehearse it until you've got it down.

Give yourself actual rest if your energy is wiped out. Scrolling on your phone doesn't restore energy. Close your eyes, go outside, or do nothing for ten minutes.

If you need to seek novelty, switch tasks and try something else for a while. You can always come back to the task later.

Fifteen Minutes or Six Hours?

Know when you're using an anti-task strategically and when it's taking over your whole day.

When you use an anti-task strategically, you're anxious about a task so you take fifteen minutes to play a game that calms you down. You feel better and go back to the task with less anxiety. Or you're exhausted and can't focus, so you watch one episode of a TV show to rest and come back to your task more alert.

When an anti-task takes over, you're anxious about a task, and play a game to avoid the anxiety. Three hours later, you're still playing, and the anxiety is worse because the deadline is creeping up on you. Or you're tired, so you turn on the TV. Now it's 10 p.m., you're still watching *Gilmore Girls*, and your chores aren't done.

Decide before you start how long you'll give it. Tell yourself you're going to scroll for 15 minutes to give yourself a break, then set a timer. When you hear the alarm, stop. If you can't, that's information, too. It means you probably need more rest than fifteen minutes can provide or the task you're avoiding is creating too much anxiety in you. Whatever it is, something needs attention before you go back to work.

If you consistently choose escape anti-tasks like cleaning or organizing when you're facing a specific type of task, that task creates anxiety for you. You'll have to learn to reduce that anxiety or get help with that type of task. I'll always have trouble making phone calls. Writing out a script when I'm not sure what to say helps. I won't say it's easy now, but it's easier, and that's made a huge difference.

If you're regularly choosing dopamine anti-tasks in the afternoon, your brain might be telling you something about when your energy is running low. The boring tasks might go better earlier in the day, when there's more in the tank.

If your go-to anti-task is rest, you probably need to raise your overall energy. Try to stick to an earlier bedtime. Fatigue is one of the first signs of dehydration. Keep your water bottle filled. Go out for a long walk when you can fit one into your day to keep your energy levels up.

Constantly choosing social anti-tasks, like calling or texting, could mean you need more human contact than your day allows. Set aside more people time instead of treating it as a reward you need to earn.

Deleting the App Doesn't Delete the Need

You've probably tried blocking your anti-tasks. You've deleted apps, installed web blockers, and left your phone in another room. It all failed to help.

The problem with that is that blocking the anti-task doesn't eliminate the need it was meeting. Delete TikTok, and you'll find another way to get that dopamine or escape. You'll constantly refresh your email. You'll decide your bookshelf needs to be reorganized by color. You'll spend two hours researching something you'll never buy. Suddenly the kitchen needs a deep cleaning.

The anti-task changes, but the need doesn't.

Consequences Don't Always Work

You do some things consistently because the consequence of not doing them is immediate and intolerable. Our greatest motivation is preventing the worst outcome from happening.

You brush your teeth because you don't want to go to work with ogre breath. You want to avoid being the subject of the breakroom gossip. You also don't want to spend thousands on dental care or have all your teeth fall out before you're old enough to collect Social Security.

You get dressed and wear clean clothes because...well, it's self-explanatory.

You eat breakfast because you don't want your stomach making ungodly sounds during your business meeting and you prefer not to pass out from low blood sugar.

But knowing the consequence doesn't always make you do the thing.

When I was in high school, I regularly ate a bag of Doritos and drank a can of Mountain Dew for lunch. Needless to say, I didn't perform at my best academic level. After the resulting sugar crash, I could have used a power nap to finish the day, but as a headstrong teenager, I didn't care that it affected me this way.

What mattered most to me was eating what I wanted. Being seen as uncool was a consequence I chose to avoid, as if I had any cool to begin with. Eating the unappetizing school lunch was the other, even though I should have been concerned with doing well in my classes. Despite what it was doing to my health and focus, I chose to accept it when everything else was telling me not to, and I paid the price for it.

Sometimes you choose one bad consequence over another.

When Nothing Bad Happens If You Don't

For tasks without immediate consequences, you need a different approach.

Exercise has vague future consequences. You won't feel the effects of not exercising for years, maybe decades. The consequence isn't immediate enough to motivate action today.

Writing your novel has no real consequence. If you never finish it, nothing bad happens. Personal disappointment isn't a consequence that drives behavior.

Learning a new skill has no deadline. You can put it off forever with no penalty.

These are the tasks where productivity advice tells you to build habits. And if you can do that, great. But you can't. So you need something else. That something else comes later in the book. Tasks with real immediate consequences are easier. When the consequence is bad enough, you're more likely to do the task.

The tasks you struggle with most are the ones where nothing bad happens if you don't do them, or where the consequences are so far away they don't feel real yet.

Ghost Habit #1

Use Your Actual Skills

You Don't Have X-ray Vision

Everyone has a skill set. This is where we need to be honest about what's in it.

People talk about the superpowers of autism, ADHD, and neurodivergence. While there are positive aspects of being neurodivergent, how are these skills useful for earning a living? Some neurodivergent people get into the right field and excel. But my so-called superpowers don't mesh well with this world. Unfortunately, this is the world I was born into.

If I were Superman, with genuine superpowers, then yes. I can see a real-world use for X-ray vision or the ability to fly. Those are highly unique, employable skills in a guy who could also handle the pressure of working in a busy downtown newsroom, which I cannot.

My ability to stare at maps for 10 hours or memorize every cast member's name in a popular movie franchise won't grant me lifelong employment, especially since I can't consistently wake up and do the same job every day. No one on LinkedIn is clamoring for my particular skill set.

So, what do people like me do?

The options you have are greater now because we're not as tied to traditional 9-to-5 employment. If you want to succeed, you sell yourself and devise a career out of the abilities you have. That's a formidable roadblock for people with minimal social skills and poor executive function. But it's possible to align your skills with the work you want to do.

Your Real Skill Set

Most productivity advice assumes you can do anything if you just try hard enough. Your real skill set is more specific than that, and knowing it is where you actually start. We all have things we're good at and things we have to admit we'll never be good at, and pretending otherwise sets you up to fail.

The times you've surprised yourself by finishing something and thought "Wait, I did that?" tell you what you are capable of. What were you doing and what was different about that day or that task?

People ask you to do things because they know you'll do it better than they could. That reveals skills you might not recognize in yourself.

It's especially the activities where time disappears. Actual productive tasks, not social media or binge-watching movies, where you look up and hours are gone. These are the tasks you can get absorbed in. You want more of these in your life.

One of my special interests is true crime cases. Once I get hooked on an intriguing story, I dig deeper and deeper. Often, I don't even realize it's been three or four hours. If I could consistently apply that level of attention to learning Japanese, I'd probably be fluent in a few months.

This is what you have. Knowing what you can do is pointless if you don't know what you're aiming for, so that's where goals come in.

Know Before You Commit

Most of us grew up hearing that we can do anything we set our hearts to. Almost every parent has told their child, "You can be anything you want to be." And that's true within reason. When you're told from your earliest memories that you can do something, and it turns out you can't or you can't without additional pain and trauma, it's unhealthy for you to hear people insist that you should be able to do it. It's damaging to instill in someone that they can do it if they try harder.

If your parents are mechanical engineers who told you all your life that math is easy, yet you can't do basic math problems without mixing up numbers, you'll be set up for disappointment if you follow in their footsteps.

The cold, hard truth is that I've always had trouble reading.

I am literate. I can comprehend words and write them, but I struggle to read full-length books. I've stared at the same page for 10 minutes, but the information doesn't sink in. If I encounter a wall of uninteresting text, my eyes twitch, and I have to reboot. It's cognitive overload because I know I'll have to read it ten times to grasp it.

That doesn't bode well for many liberal arts majors, where you may only be engrossed in a fraction of the texts you're required to read. In college, I had no choice but to skim the readings and rely on summaries, hoping to absorb enough main points to pass the exams.

I couldn't understand what was wrong. My IQ test said I was intelligent. My schools placed me in gifted programs, but I couldn't do what seemed the easiest thing. Read a single book, cover to cover. I had a near photographic memory, which compensated for my reading deficit for most of my childhood. That eventually caught up with me in high school, when the workload increased, and my grades fell.

I should have chosen a college major more aligned with my abilities. Had someone recognized my neurodivergent conditions in childhood, I could have been steered into subjects with less reading and writing and into areas that held my interest better.

Remember those kids who sat in the back, head down, hoping not to be noticed when the teacher asked for volunteers to read out loud? If I were chosen, I'd shake and stutter, while the other kids would snicker at my disastrous attempt.

It wasn't that I couldn't read. In my head, I spoke with perfect diction, but what came out sounded like the unintelligible adult voices in the *Peanuts* cartoons. Whatever value the teacher found in that lesson left me traumatized. I had one more disturbing memory to relive in my head every night.

No amount of practice can change the fact that the signals don't always go from your brain to your mouth as intended. Sometimes the wires get crossed somewhere between thinking and speaking, and what comes out isn't what you intended. Other times, your mind is already ten steps ahead, working on the next thought before the first one has finished. And sometimes your senses are overwhelmed, your mind goes blank, and you freeze. If your reality were similar, you know the fear that overtakes you.

And yet, people think it's within our control, and we willingly choose not to change it. In reality, it slowly erodes our confidence and self-esteem.

When I was young, people told me I was smart. Smart people can pick up a book and read it, so what was wrong with me? I thought I was a failure.

Your difficulties with reading, numbers, language, judging time, or communication don't reflect your worth or intelligence.

It's easy to feel bad when you can't do something that seems simple for everyone else. No one should push you into doing things that will cause you mental anguish. It's not their call. When you follow their advice, you're left to pick up the pieces when it doesn't work out.

After college, I stumbled around for a while, working temp jobs and trying to decide what I'd like to do with the next 40 or so years of my life. With no clear direction, I made the bold move to apply to the local sheriff's department.

Yes, really.

At the time, it sounded like a great idea. Excitement, danger. Well, not so much, as there was little action going on in my small farming community. My dreams didn't care. Fueled by a passion for justice and way too many buddy cop movies, I would keep my tiny part of the world safe from the bad guys.

There was no way I'd pass the initial job testing. My background on paper, as a fresh college grad, looked stronger than most, but they couldn't see I was an introvert with poor organizational skills who rarely made eye contact and hated to drive.

Yet, somehow, I thought I was the next supercop ready to take on the criminal underworld. Dreaming big is admirable, but you need to dream realistically.

That career was all wrong for me. I probably could have worked in the IT department, had one existed, but strapping on a sidearm and doing 90 miles an hour on the back country roads wasn't the career for me.

If everything comes together, you can succeed, but saying you want to be the next CEO of a multi-billion-dollar startup won't happen for even .01% of us. Keep your goals realistic.

If you've managed to get hired and stay employed at a job you enjoy, you're ahead of the game.

Not Every Dream Is the Right Dream

Society pushes us to find the perfect career much too early in life. Often, we lack sufficient life experience or a strong support system to lead us to our best path.

Yes, you can do almost anything, but will it lead to a fulfilling life? Unless you're prepared to dread waking up to the same monotonous life, think hard about your abilities.

If you haven't found your niche yet, focus on the things you can do. Your goals should be practical, even on a small scale. Don't rush into jobs that aren't suited to you because you think it's the "right" thing to do by society's standards.

I enjoy cooking, so I've often considered opening a restaurant at different points in my life. But each time I'm reminded that it's beyond my abilities. As much as I love to experiment with new foods and flavors, I don't have the temperament to run a restaurant.

I imagine it would be an exciting experience at times, but without the insane dedication to grueling hours in a steaming-hot kitchen, the dream wouldn't last long for me. Running a restaurant means dealing with constant problems on the fly, customers' finicky tastes, and regularly taking savage reviews on the chin. The fast pace and potentially irate patrons would drain every ounce of my passion for cooking within a few months.

It's not within my skill set to go all in and open my own restaurant, but I could share my love of food by creating a YouTube channel, starting a blog, or launching an artisanal food business on a much smaller scale. Whatever your interest, you can bring it down to a level that meets your ability and increases your chances of success.

It's Not Gone, It's Waiting

If you try something new and discover you aren't interested or it's not within your abilities, move on.

As children, many of us were taught not to give up on the things we started. Maybe you were forced to take piano lessons for years after your love for it wore off. Was it beneficial? For some, probably. Perhaps you're grateful your parents wouldn't let you drop it. Maybe it carried through your whole life, or you found renewed interest in it years later.

But there's another group that, had they been able to nix the piano lessons, would have excelled at the French horn, jiu-jitsu, or snowboarding.

Just because you start a new project, interest, or activity doesn't mean you have to stick with it. This is outdated thinking today. It probably won't work out in the long run if it's not right for you anyway. Save yourself the trouble.

If you drop a project that still interests you, stash it away for later. Write it down in a list of activities or skills you want to resume. There's no rule saying you can't come back to it. Now may not be the right time in your life to take up kayaking or learning to code in Python, but maybe it will be down the road. You may return to it someday when you have better resources, more time, or more motivation to stay with it.

Stop Letting the Bullies Live Rent-Free

Your past does not define your future. That's hard to believe when we've been conditioned to think we are less than others because of our additional challenges. We believe that to achieve great things, we need a proven track record behind us, and that our CVs, recommendations, social networks, and employment history are the tickets to our future success. If we don't have those things, we fear we're missing something everyone else has.

Yes, we have different abilities and backgrounds, but that doesn't make us less worthy. We have overcome much more than most people. Our past experience, especially the adversity we've endured and overcome, isn't reflected on paper or in a PDF. Your ability to keep picking yourself up and taking the next difficult step is a strength others can't always see.

When you were young, getting called the weird kid or the r-word was hurtful. You might have been the class clown people laughed at instead of with, or the invisible cafeteria loner. I transferred in for my senior year and spent it eating lunch in the hallway so I wouldn't have to set foot in the cafeteria. I'm not sure I ever found out where it was.

Some of that damage runs deeper than any book can reach. If that's where you are, talking to someone who understands neurodivergence is worth your time.

We take other people's opinions too much to heart. Other people don't hold you back. You hold yourself back by internalizing their hateful words. Their opinions don't define you unless you let them. That's a "them" problem.

As we get older and those days slip further into time, we gain self-confidence and can better separate ourselves from the past. That's where it should stay. You are in control today. Giving those memories free rent in your head today is letting the bullies hurt you all over again, and that's not acceptable.

Whatever place you are in life, you won't be there forever. You can deliberately change it today, or if you tough it out long enough, it'll change on its own.

Thinking About It Is Not Doing It

It's a giant leap from thought to action. Thinking is safe and comfortable, but taking action is scary and uncertain. Several times, I've wanted to make a major change. I wanted to chuck it all out and start down a new road. Implementing those changes took years. I wasn't willing to put in all the effort necessary to change my life yet.

I was willing to plan, research, dream, and devote my brainpower to it, but I wasn't prepared to take action and make it happen. Even though I'd lie awake at night, dreaming about how much better my life would be if I did it, I procrastinated and made excuses.

Even minor changes won't happen without some shift or upheaval in your life.

With all your knowledge today, what is the best decision you can make right now?

If we ask ourselves this question whenever we need to take action, we won't make rash decisions, and we won't look back regretting that we didn't examine all options. It may not turn out to be the correct one, but it wasn't because we didn't give it full consideration.

It's time for dinner. Should I eat a big, healthy salad or a giant bowl of ice cream with whipped cream and sprinkles?

The library is three blocks away. Should I drive or walk?

I've been working hard on a project that's due first thing in the morning. Should I put in an hour of overtime today to make sure it's done well while it's all fresh in my mind? Or should I plan to come in early tomorrow to finish it and hope nothing goes wrong?

We know the right answer to all three. We also know which one we're going to pick. The easy choice is fine occasionally. When it's always the easy choice, things get harder and stay harder.

When it comes to bigger life choices, you can't hold yourself responsible for facts you don't know yet. Unless we're psychically gifted, we don't have a crystal ball that tells us all the possible outcomes and scenarios. We've got to depend on our knowledge and observations to make the best decision at any given moment. That's all anyone can ask of you.

***

Quick Take

- Know what you can do on your worst days. That's your real skill set.
- The tasks where time disappears tell you where your abilities are.
- Stop trying to fit yourself into roles built around skills you don't have.
- Dream realistically.
- Your past doesn't define what you can do next.

Ghost Habit #2

Set Your Goals

You Need Something to Aim For

Without a goal, none of this goes anywhere. Every great project, invention, business venture, or event that's ever been done started as an idea. It was nothing but a thought until someone plucked it out of the ether, put it into motion, and followed it through to completion. An idea that someone threw out at a meeting. A thought scribbled in a notebook. Something a friend suggested that sparked their curiosity. A dream you had one night.

How do we turn a thought into a finished product? It must become a goal.

If you struggle to get out of bed in the morning and can barely do the things you need to survive, showering and eating regular meals must be among your first goals. With time, you'll get better at this, but for now, cover the basics first.

Once you have that down, you can add more to your day, like shopping or exercising. You can look beyond daily living activities to get to a more self-sufficient place. If you're unable to hold a job, go to school, or engage in meaningful daily activities, this should be your next goal. You need something to work toward while keeping your goals achievable.

I struggled most in the days before you could tap into your phone app and order up some food. I spent my days in grungy sweatpants and worn college t-shirts. All I have to do now is shuffle to my front door in my fuzzy slippers to pick up the bag of food. Back in the dark ages, we didn't have that. I had to get out of my warm bed and pop something edible into the microwave.

I didn't have many goals. I needed to sleep and pacify myself so I wouldn't think about how bad my life was. I was truly a **NEET**, Not in Employment, Education, or Training. Along with the piles of unwashed laundry, a rapidly depleting bank account, and past-due payment notices, I had enough anxiety that I could barely function.

My finances were a mess. On top of my steadily increasing student loan balance, I had tens of thousands of dollars in credit card debt, with no foreseeable way to repay any of it. The odds were stacked against me. Job opportunities in my area were scarce beyond factory and minimum-wage retail jobs, which were impossible for me to do.

My hat's off to the people in fast food or customer service jobs who can put out 10 fires at once and get paid next to nothing for their time. I'd been let go or burnt out and quit enough times to know those jobs were no longer an option for me.

I couldn't go to the doctor then because "no job = no healthcare" in America. With each new bill that hit my mailbox, the pressure mounted, and the despair compounded.

When people talked about reaching the bottom of the barrel, I knew what that was like. That was the lowest of the lows. I was all too familiar with the desperation and sleepless nights that kept me spiraling further down. I knew the intrusive thoughts swirling in my head every night just before I mercifully drifted off to sleep. I felt the never-ending cycle of worry, coupled with the dire financial reality of my situation, each fueling the other.

It's hard to feel hope when you only see your life as a long road of more of the same. It couldn't go on like this forever. But the question was, could I fix it before it came crashing down on its own?

Not everyone experiences it to this extreme degree. Sometimes, we have short bouts of this, when we'd rather stay in bed and do nothing to put off our problems for a while. But we get over it relatively quickly. Confronting your problems is unavoidable. The longer you wait to confront your issues, the worse your conditions get and the harder it is to get out of the chaos.

Your baseline goals, the ones that keep you functional day to day, are your non-negotiables.

The Non-Negotiables

The next step is to ensure you meet your obligations and responsibilities. There are fixed obligations you need to do daily or almost daily. At the times you're at your most unfocused and can barely leave your bedroom, the tasks that keep you and those around you safe and healthy are the things that you take care of first. Direct your energy to those. Everything else will have to wait.

Some fixed obligations are the no-brainers we'll discuss later, like:

- Eating and staying hydrated
- Sleeping
- Showering
- Taking required medication
- Caring for anyone who depends on you
- Getting some physical activity
- Having enough income to cover the basics

If we don't feel up to doing these things, our goal is to do what we can to get them done by using the strategies in this book. This is the minimum effort we need to make. The last thing we want to do is spend extra time redoing them. Not doing them at all harms our health and can set us back even further.

Keeping a water bottle with you all day, setting an alarm or an email reminder to take medication, keeping healthy foods nearby, and having a friend remind you can all help.

Sometimes it's hard for us to distinguish what's necessary and what can be put off. Maybe you can look at a pile of dirty dishes and put them off, but eventually, you'll have to do them. What's necessary for a basic, healthy life has to come first.

After we address these, we can move on to our flexible obligations, which drastically improve our lives but may not be required or may change regularly. We do them as they come up. While you may worry about these for weeks or months, doing them quickly and competently improves your life.

Getting in the right mindset for these is challenging when you're completely uninterested, but doing them is for your benefit, things like:

- Studying for a test
- Updating a budget
- Mowing the lawn
- Paying bills
- Scheduling an appointment

- Doing a home repair
- Attending a meeting
- Making a difficult phone call

If you can meet your flexible obligations with less friction, your quality of life will improve. If you could study more, you could get a better job. You may get a raise or promotion if you can complete additional work tasks. If you could take on more chores, you might feel better about your home, which could increase your self-confidence.

Every task we complete leads to the next, and we get the same choice each time. Keep going, stall, or stop.

Beyond our obligations are the things we want to do, the non-essential tasks that greatly enrich our lives. They are not required, but without some of them, we won't be living our best lives. They are activities such as:

- Spending time on a hobby
- Hanging with friends
- Going out to dinner at a nice restaurant
- Taking a personal development class
- Going to movies, sports, or cultural events

- Training for a new career
- Traveling
- Completing extra projects for fun or side income

Most of these activities aren't hard for us to find the energy to do. We can play hours of video games, talk to friends, or catch a game without much thought.

When we're enthusiastic about a new idea, signing up for a class or planning to start a home business may be easy. Unfortunately, if we do our wants first, we may not have the time or mental energy to complete our obligations.

The tasks we need help remembering or completing go on the **Task List** (covered in Ghost Habit #4).

Tasks vs. Projects

Every day, we have a list of tasks we should do. Read the news, prepare lunch, drive to work, walk the dog, answer emails, and schedule a dentist appointment. We also have projects or a series of single-step tasks to complete. Plan a trip, set up an event, prepare a work presentation, and research a new business we'd like to start.

Cleaning out an overstuffed walk-in closet is, at the very least, a half-day project. Many small, often unrelated tasks make up one big project. Empty your closet. Sort through boxes and decide what to throw away, sell, donate, or keep. Take your trash to the landfill if it's too much for your weekly pickup. Drop off your donations. Go to the store to buy new clothes hangers, bins, or boxes. Sweep, do any repairs, and install new shelves. Repack and label everything and return it to its new place.

A task can be done quickly and is likely to be finished in one session if we want to. I use the word "project" for actions comprised of multiple tasks that may take many hours, days, weeks, or more.

The Two Major Questions

When you're contemplating what to do with your time, most of what you should do can be summed up in two questions.

1. Am I doing something productive at the moment?
2. What can I do right now to make life easier for myself later?

If you answer yes to the first question, proceed with that task. If the answer is no, consider two additional points. Do you have enough focus right now? And what tasks fit where you are?

You're excited because it's two days before your much-anticipated weekend getaway, but you haven't done anything all day. You're vegging out on the couch with *The Obscenely Wealthy Debutantes of Sunny City* blaring from your TV.

Ask yourself if you're doing something productive. The answer is no, you're binge-watching TV, which is not an efficient use of your time. But can you focus on doing something? Yes, marginally. Tasks like cleaning don't take much concentration to complete.

Channeling your anxious energy into productive tasks like running errands, washing laundry, or tidying up while you're waiting to leave will ensure you come home to a clean, inviting space with extra time to unwind. No one wants to glumly walk in the door because your return to work is imminent, only to face a pile of chores waiting for you.

Pick One Goal

Most people with ADHD try to work on 10 goals at once, and that's where everything falls apart.

You can have 10 goals. There's nothing wrong with that. Want to lose weight, start a YouTube channel, learn to play guitar, train for a marathon, and declutter your house? It probably won't go the way you want. Two weeks later, you've made zero progress on any of them and feel like a failure again.

Having goals is not the problem. Taking on too many at once is. Your brain can't actively pursue 10 goals simultaneously. You can add one, maybe two if they're small and unrelated.

So when you decide to add a new goal, add one. Not five. Write it down and give it your focus before you consider adding another. Put it somewhere you'll see it, like a sticky note or your phone. That's your new active goal.

The rest of your goals should be written down somewhere and marked as "not right now." They're still goals, and you're not abandoning them, but they're not on your plate this week. Stay with the goal until you're making progress, it's done, or until it's not working for you.

It feels like you should be doing more. But chasing too many new goals leads to overwhelm, which leads to paralysis, which means nothing gets done at all. One completed goal beats 10 goals that you start and abandon.

You've picked your new goal. Now plan for the part where it doesn't go the way you expected, because it won't. Every goal needs a contingency, because things will go wrong.

Always Have a Backup Plan

Every wrong turn is a learning experience. We will face problems in life. That's a given. Since we know we'll struggle, we need to cushion our fall when things go wrong. You need a backup plan.

Like every Hollywood action thriller where the good guy almost saves the day but gets thwarted at every turn, there's always a twist that keeps your goal out of reach. I've never had unbelievable luck where every task I start goes smoothly. It hasn't happened to this point in my life, so why would it begin now?

What will I do if I don't get that business loan? I'll investigate alternative funding.

What happens if I don't pass that certification exam? I'll study more and try again.

What if they don't think I'm the best candidate for the job I want? I'll revise my CV, get some new certifications, and get an even better job.

What if my side gig never makes a dime? I'll rework my product and change up my marketing plan.

When you fall short, and you will fall short, that's a guarantee, it can seem soul-crushing when you've worked really hard toward your goal and still failed.

It feels worse than when your 7th-grade crush very publicly rebuffed you at your junior high dance.

You can recover from a failed business, a low GPA, financial debt, or a poor personal decision. Very few people can say they've always made the best decision when it mattered most. Likewise, most of us will admit we have more than one regret.

When things don't work out, use the **Restart Rule**.

The Restart Rule

You fail out of school. You get fired. Your business never gets off the ground. When that happens, you have two options. You can give up or you can keep going. The Restart Rule is one way to do that.

1. Regroup. Take an impartial look at your situation.

2. Refocus. Reassess how you could do things differently.

3. Return. Throw yourself back in and try again.

The first part of the Restart Rule is to take an unbiased look at your entire situation. Do you enjoy this subject, career, or project? How did your strengths and weaknesses affect it? Did factors that you had no control over play a part in the failure? Be honest because the next steps depend on what you decide here.

The second step is to reassess how you could do things differently. Where did things go wrong? Can you get additional advice or training? Get help if you need it and figure out how you'd change things up the second time around.

Once you've determined what you want to do, the last step is to throw yourself back in and try again. Apply to a related program. Interview for a similar job. Give your side business another try with the new knowledge you've acquired. You're not coming at it as a rookie this time.

That's been my M.O. in life. Pick up and start again.

One of the more notable times was when my company shut down, leaving me and several hundred others without a job. This was a career-type job with low turnover, where most employees had 20 or 30 years in and retired from. I'd spent three years trying to get that job. I thought it might be my forever job, too.

That prospect ended on a random workday. Someone from "upstairs" dropped off a single-page memo to our supervisor. Within minutes, the news was buzzing throughout the million-square-foot building. Our location was closing at the end of the month.

They gave us three choices. Take your severance and find your own job, along with five hundred other people. Try to transfer to a facility in another state. Or take two years of paid job retraining.

I had to look at it honestly. I was already looking to leave that job. A job transfer only makes sense financially if everything goes perfectly and there's an opening for another job you like and are eligible for.

Most of the older workers didn't want to start over. I did.

I didn't make a career out of that new training, but I learned skills I couldn't have afforded otherwise, made friends that lasted, and my next job built on that education. I'd make the same choice again.

The retraining covered tuition and living expenses, but it was less than half what I'd been making. The student loans I'd been chipping away at went back to minimum payments and stayed there.

Had I known how quickly things can go from "everything's ok" to "your job just went bye-bye," I would have saved more money and not gotten so comfortable with the regular paycheck.

Though it's not a comforting thought at the moment, a hidden benefit of each failure is that we have a lesser chance of failure the next time it happens.

Perfectionism will try to stop you. Negative thoughts will tell you you're not good enough. External pressure will make you feel like you're falling behind your peers. Things will go wrong.

None of that means you stop trying.

The Chance You Didn't Plan For

People are afraid to go back to school as older adults, which is understandable when you don't have much in common with the current college-age crowd. But universities have significantly changed their approach, especially since the pandemic. Online classes that work within your schedule are easier than ever. If you can hammer out the finances, there's no better time to go back.

People hesitate anyway. They think they're too old or won't fit in, their friends and family will think they're foolish, or the diploma won't matter anymore.

But what does matter? If it's important to you, that's reason enough.

You're 40 and considering going back to get your bachelor's degree. You think, "I'm too old. I'll be nearly 45 when I graduate from college." So, you put it off. Either way, in five years, you will be 45. Would you rather be 45 with or without that diploma?

The same advice applies to people of any age. 35, 55, or 75+. If you want to do it, then find a way.

My father has often told me how proud he was of his father, who returned to finish high school in his 50s. Like many young men at the time, he left school early to support his family. While it's hard to believe in our current economic climate, there was an almost mythical time when a single lower-middle-class income could comfortably support a family.

Outside of the evening classes he attended, he spent every night for months studying in a drab basement office space. At the same desk where he kept the books for his plumbing business, he did algebra and read English poetry.

Returning to finish an education wasn't easy at that time. Students only had the option of in-person evening classes. My grandfather also felt the additional stigma of being an "old" person returning to school. Now, it's almost expected to see middle-aged adults back in the classroom.

You may not realize it, but your actions speak volumes to those who care about you. My grandfather earned his diploma, the whole family was proud of him, and many decades later, we still tell the story.

If the opportunity is there and you want it, take it. Every day you wait is a day you didn't start. They add up fast. You can't change your core personality or become a different person, but you can polish the edges. All the days you struggled have taught you that if it were easy to change, it would have happened by sheer will alone.

You've got your goals figured out. Now here's where traditional productivity advice would tell you to build habits, create routines, wake up at 5 a.m., and stick to a rigid schedule. We can ghost it all.

***

Quick Take

- Add one new goal at a time. Adding ten at once means finishing none.
- Cover your non-negotiables first. Everything else waits.
- Write your active goal somewhere you'll see it.
- Mark the rest as "not right now," not abandoned.
- When it falls apart, use the Restart Rule and start again.
- If an opportunity you want appears, take it.

Ghost Habit #3

You Don't Need Habits

Same Advice, Same Result

Eating dinner isn't a habit. Neither is sleeping, or showering, or getting dressed. You do those things because your body demands them or your life requires them. Nobody tracks those on a habit app. Nobody loses their streak for eating a late lunch.

The habits the productivity gurus are selling are different. They want you to build morning routines, exercise schedules, meditation, and journaling habits from nothing, maintain them through willpower, and track them obsessively, or they fall apart. Miss a day, and you're starting over. When life gets hard, it all collapses.

Those are the habits you don't need.

For years, I'd read the same advice about improving my life, whether it was the fixation on building habits, scrupulously following a daily routine, carving my days into time blocks, or any of the many popular productivity strategies. After a while, whenever I stumbled on the latest, greatest end-all solution that would finally fix me, I'd think, "Here we go again."

I desperately wanted to find a way to improve myself. Yet, none of it fixed me. It wasn't that it was too difficult to understand or the steps too hard to follow, but the advice didn't work with my abilities.

It took years to realize that my life has long been habit-free, routine-free, and discipline-free. That goes squarely against the popular advice. For many of us, habits, routines, and discipline don't stick, and there is another way.

If any of these productivity strategies work for you, keep using them. Don't dump something that's helping because someone else tells you to. This chapter is for people who have tried these strategies repeatedly and watched them fall apart every time. If you're exhausted from forcing routines that never hold, if you feel broken because you can't do what everyone says you should do, stop trying. You can't produce consistency on command, and no amount of trying harder will change that.

One habit I've tried to build many times is leaving the kitchen counters completely clutter-free so I can wake up to a spotless kitchen. I've tried more times than I can count. It's probably easy if you love to clean. I do love to cook, though, and I have too many kitchen tools and gadgets. Somehow the mail ends up on the counters. And the trio of coffee cups I rotate between. The headphones I set down somewhere. The things I walk into the kitchen with, forget about, and never walk back out with. The takeout salt-and-pepper packets and the paper towels that didn't make it back into their holder.

I love the feeling of pouring my first morning coffee in a bright, clean kitchen. I can't keep it up, so I stopped trying to make it a habit. On the days I can't do it, I live with it.

Dump the Productivity Advice That Doesn't Work

I won't tell you that popular productivity strategies are all a waste of your time. You'll find people who swear by them. They can micro-schedule their weeks, check off every task they set out to do, and get more done in one day than I can in my most productive week.

The ones that don't work for most of us are the usual suspects. Habits and routines, time blocking, the **Pomodoro Technique**, reward systems, and the 1% improvement myth. They require too much energy to execute. Maintaining your newly found habits is practically a full-time job for severely distracted and mentally exhausted people. The reward doesn't outweigh the substantial effort required.

Who Needs Habits?

Every activity you want to do doesn't have to become a habit. There are activities I like to do regularly that don't need to attain the exalted "habit" status.

The productivity gurus define a habit as something so automatic that it requires almost no conscious thought. You see a cue in your environment, you respond automatically, you don't even have to decide. That's what they're selling. Do it enough times and it becomes ingrained in you.

Habit is easily the most overhyped word in the productivity sphere. Consistently inconsistent people like us will rarely get there, and when the habit collapses, we're back to zero with one more failure on the list.

They are ghost habits to me because they don't exist.

You could argue that brushing my teeth in the morning, at night before bed, and, much to the disapproval of my dentist, less frequently at midday is a habit. Or putting on a seatbelt when I get in the car is a habit. They are far from ingrained actions that I can do without thought.

People have told me I have speech patterns that could be classified as habits, as well as my daily activities like eating, sleeping, bathing, and dressing.

These aren't actions I want to change or even perceive myself doing, so they are not the "habits" the hustle bros promote.

Likewise, clocking in at 7:59 a.m. to work because my job forces me to be there by 8 is not a habit.

None of these are my habits. I brush my teeth daily, but it's not something I do automatically. It's not as though I see that it's 7 a.m. or 9 p.m. and instantly drop whatever I'm doing, turn, and robotically walk, arms extended, to my bathroom sink to brush my teeth. And yes, I do put on my seatbelt immediately most of the time because I think about it, but a few times a week, I get a block down the street before the warning alarm scolds me.

I eat, sleep, shower, and work because my body demands it or my life requires it. Those are part of being human, not habits I created.

Why Habit Tracking Backfires

Yet people take it one step further, meticulously tracking their fledgling habits daily. Habit tracking to create or break habits requires time, focus, and dedication, three things that are in short supply in my world.

If you want to start a positive habit, you imagine how your days will improve once you incorporate it. You begin with gusto because you're intent on sticking with it. Then it gets substantially more difficult after a few days or weeks of marking Xs in your chart.

There's some element of forcing yourself to continue the habit. You're told you need willpower to stay consistent and continue when your motivation wanes. That's hardly a recipe for success.

When you're trying to cut carbs, preparing your own meals at home makes it easier. But when you attend a party or go out to dinner with friends, and the baskets of breadsticks hit the table, is your habit tracker enough?

I've always had a bad "habit" of biting my fingernails. I don't want to do it, but it's difficult to kick when I'm anxious. I can stop for a while, but I might fall back into it when I get nervous. If I tracked this, writing it down or checking a box in an app would mean nothing. That doesn't enter my mind when I feel the urge to bite.

Discipline is forcing yourself to do something that may damage you in other ways. Hustle culture tells us that if we don't behave correctly, we deserve to be punished. There's nothing productive about running yourself into the ground with a productivity label slapped on it.

In theory, even the most time-challenged and scatterbrained person has the physical ability to adhere to a rigid schedule, but it's not the best course of action if it hinders your progress and harms your mental health. It's winning a battle but setting yourself up to lose the war.

The Routine Problem

After establishing habits, people want to incorporate them into their daily routines. It keeps their lives orderly and productive, and this order carries over into a calmer and less stressful life.

When people think of following a routine, they commonly imagine something like a morning routine where you wake up at a particular time and complete a list of activities in a set order. Waking up, making your bed, showering, dressing, meditating, checking your messages, making coffee, and eating breakfast.

The hustle bros and productivity gurus are obsessed with creating a flawless morning routine. They'll insist that you need that consistency in your life and that rigorous adherence to a daily routine will supposedly magnify your productivity and lay the groundwork for incredible success. And if you can't do it, well, then you're obviously lazy and not making enough of an effort.

You're usually a night owl who sleeps in until 10 a.m., but you've devised an ideal morning routine to kickstart the new and improved you. You'll wake up at 5 a.m. every Monday through Friday and go straight to the gym to work out. At 6:30, you'll have 20 minutes to make your ultra-nutritious banana kale spirulina smoothie. After that, you'll meditate, then at 7:15 a.m., you'll sit down to read the latest news in fitness, investing, and generating passive income. At 8, you'll start your workday by doing some totally life-changing self-improvement courses.

But how realistic is it to maintain if it's not something you're 100% ready to take on? You don't know today how well you'll be functioning at 6 a.m. tomorrow, three days from now, or a month from now, but because you have a new routine, you'll know exactly where you're supposed to be every minute for the first four hours each day.

How likely are you to make such a drastic change to your mornings? What you think you can do and what you will do can be two very contradictory things.

This is why routines often don't work for neurodivergent individuals. Like habits, they may be hard to maintain temporarily until we burn out. Being glued to the clock is a stifling concept for people who are consistently inconsistent and love newness and flexibility. Routine creates worry and anxiety because it forces us to expend energy thinking about when, where, and how to do a task.

As a result, I don't have a morning routine. While I have daily tasks, they don't always follow the same sequence or take the same amount of time. My daily morning tasks are like my favorite Spotify playlist. I don't listen to it at the same time, in the same order, or to the same number of songs. I choose what I want to hear when I feel like it. Taking that approach lets me get things done without wasting energy on everything else.

There's a great deal in our lives that we have no control over. When something comes up unexpectedly, like a work or school schedule change, a work trip, a breakup, a move, graduation, an unexpected family situation, or even getting saddle sores from the hundreds of miles you put on your spin bike, it throws your routine out the window.

Some don't have a set routine. Every day is different, and we thrive on that flexibility. We don't go to sleep or wake up at the same time. Either way, we still have our informal list of activities to do. Getting out of bed, showering, brushing our teeth, putting on clothes, getting the kids ready for school, eating cereal, and walking the dog. We can also incorporate other activities into our mornings, like yoga, reading, breathing exercises, and cleaning.

If you need to be in your car by 7:30 to get to work on time, for most tasks, it doesn't matter what order you do them in. You do the ones you absolutely need to do for that day.

Decades of trying and failing have proven that scheduling, tracking, and adhering to a routine don't work for me. I can't stick with anything for any significant length of time if it doesn't come naturally to me. Since rejecting most of the popular strategies, my life has turned around.

Am I still distracted, anxious, unfocused, and unmotivated at times? Of course. I may see the proverbial shiny thing, and my focus is M.I.A. I've come to realize this is my nature. I accept it's what I am, I work around it, and I no longer criticize myself for it.

People say it's the journey that's important, but that's not entirely true. Habits and routines that eat up my time and erode my self-esteem with one failure after another aren't getting me anywhere.

The reward doesn't exceed the effort and frustration required.

The 1% Improvement Myth

Productivity gurus emphasize making small, positive daily changes, which they claim will lead to substantial gains in productivity. The idea is a 1% improvement every single day until it adds up to something significant.

Anyone who's learned a musical instrument knows that practicing 30 minutes a day improves one's skill faster than cramming for three hours only on Sundays. That's true. The problem is that the 1% improvement myth turns that idea into a daily obligation. Every single day, you have to be measurably better than yesterday. One step forward, two steps back doesn't count. The days you can barely function don't count. The weeks where life falls apart don't count. For people whose progress has never moved in a straight line, it's a guarantee of failure.

It's true. Minor changes add up over time. The problem is the pressure of doing it every day. It takes some of us an enormous effort to stay consistent enough to put them into practice, and we can't stick with it, so our improvement isn't linear.

Set your goals and move toward them when you can, without measuring every day against the last. That's how we function.

Some days you can barely focus. On other days you hyperfocus. Some days you get ahead, some days you slide back. It's like a game of Chutes and Ladders you played as a kid. You'll be elated when you do more than you expected, then disappointed in yourself on the days you don't. The inconsistency is what leads to frustration because you can't keep a steady pace.

Other times, we need to take a break and hold the line to sustain our momentum. When we've rested and regrouped, we move forward again.

Taking far more time than you think it should is still vastly superior to doing nothing or something that will cause you to lose ground. Don't work against yourself. We get more done when working on tasks we actually want to do.

The Pomodoro Technique

You've probably tried Pomodoro. Most people with ADHD have. It's near the top of the list of most popular productivity strategies.

Productivity gurus, CEOs, and even celebrities swear by it. Working in short increments seems helpful, in theory. Even so, it's a simple concept that can be difficult for people like us to put into practice.

If you've tried to incorporate the Pomodoro Technique and haven't seen positive results, it's not surprising. That short break is an ample opportunity to get pulled into an anti-task and put off doing the next session.

Pomodoro is like attending an in-person class. It forces learning and concentration at a set time, creating an artificial rhythm that doesn't work for people who are essentially time-challenged.

Your attention is on the timer, not the work you're doing. You're looking at the clock or thinking about how many minutes you have left. Besides the break, there's no incentive to use your time efficiently. I can do 25 minutes now or later. It doesn't matter. The only immediate benefit is checking it off my **Task List**.

If you finally get absorbed in your work, taking a mandatory break is the last thing you should do. You've found your focus. Stay in it.

If it doesn't work for you, you're not alone. There's a similar concept behind time blocking. It's difficult to force yourself to work on a task when you're not ready to focus.

By definition, Pomodoros give us rules to follow, and if you disregard them and start and stop work when you naturally feel like it, it's no longer a Pomodoro.

Rewards and Bribes

Rewards may not always be effective, but they can be if they hold meaning for you. You want that pot of gold at the end of the rainbow. You can withhold fun activities until you complete a less desirable task. For some, rewards are an incentive to complete the task.

It's the same logic as not letting a child leave the dinner table until they've eaten their peas. The child chokes down the peas, earns their freedom to leave the table, and never learns to like peas.

We can take rewards a step further and turn our tasks into games, since we're all about seeking out that dopamine. Many of us do appreciate a challenge. Making it a game can create interest in a task you'd otherwise loathe.

Make it into a simple game. Hang up your clean clothes, earn a reward. Hang up your clothes for an entire week, and earn an upgraded reward. Or up the ante and create a points structure for your tasks.

A common approach is to assign points to tasks and earn rewards when you hit set daily targets. Get bigger rewards when you hit the target for a fixed number of days.

If you want to make it even easier, several apps "gamify" your tasks. You add your tasks, earn points, and receive rewards for completing them. Earn more points based on difficulty level, duration, or how much you enjoy (or don't enjoy) doing them.

The game is only effective when the win motivates you to do your tasks. If it motivates you, use it. If it doesn't, you're not missing anything.

Time Blocking

One productivity method I tried while in school was time blocking. I'd dutifully write out my schedule for the next week, assigning my important tasks a chunk of time to accomplish maximum output each day. I had it all figured out.

My daily schedule was supposed to look something like this.

8–9 a.m. Texts/Emails

9–10 a.m. Social media/Website

10 a.m.–12 p.m. Reading/Class time

12–1 p.m. Break
1–2 p.m. Reading/Class Time
2–4 p.m. Writing
4–5 p.m. Admin Work

It was a disaster. I usually felt like the cryptkeeper when my alarm went off at 7 a.m. or I was instantly awake and chipper at 4:30 a.m., having already downed three cups of coffee by the time the alarm buzzed. I'd get sidetracked looking at random websites. Answering a single email would take an hour, further delaying things. Often, my wi-fi would fizzle out. As the morning went on, I could hardly stay awake watching videos of professors reading their tired lectures from 20 years ago with all the enthusiasm of a city zoning board meeting.

The real problem was my **time blindness**.

That Took How Long?

Time blindness is an all-too-common problem that undermines our ability to time-block. We may finish the task quickly if we can focus on it during the designated hours, leaving us extra time we're likely to squander. We can get so absorbed in it that we won't realize we've sailed right past the deadline. Or, if we're not interested in the task, it won't get done at all.

It's hard to judge the length of any task when you don't understand time. We can't accurately estimate how long our project will take or how much time we should allocate. I can only judge time by how long it's taken me in the past to complete the same project, and that can vary widely depending on the conditions. Things rarely go exactly the same way twice.

Someone who works 30 minutes at a time, if forced to work by the clock, will probably stare at the screen, tap their pen, scribble in their notebook, think about what to make for dinner, watch the birds outside, and then remember that they need to pick up the mail. They might rearrange their desktop icons and eventually open the PDF they should be reading. They think it's only taken a few minutes, but are surprised to find they have 10 minutes of work time left.

Alternatively, like Pomodoros, when you're consciously aware of the clock, it's agonizing to know you have a set amount of time to complete a task, and you can never find your rhythm.

Time blocking is a skill I'd love to activate, but my focus level or temperament rarely aligns with the scheduled blocks when I need it to. Blocking out time in designated increments is counterproductive for unfocused minds and increases stress when it involves a heavy task that requires full concentration.

Time blocking also doesn't work well when dealing with clients or coworkers. You can't end a phone or video call or stop working on a complex project because the time for that block has run out. You might be at peak productivity when it's up. It's important not to disrupt the momentum when you're deep into a project.

Likewise, you can't time-block others from interrupting you, whether with coworkers at the office or family or roommates with "just one quick question." What seems like a quick chat can throw your schedule completely off.

Can It Be Time Blocked?

Even for people who can't normally do time blocking, it can work well for some tasks, though not the ones the productivity gurus tell us.

Time blocking works best for required events like doctor's appointments or work meetings because they're often out of our hands. While you don't know exactly how long you'll be sitting in a waiting room or how long your boss will drone on about the sales numbers, you can err on the side of caution and overestimate. We're still on track if it goes beyond.

Time blocking can also be effective for rote tasks like cleaning or laundry. You don't have to feel inspired to do those activities. The only requirement is that you start and finish it. Your head doesn't have to be in a game as much as it does with writing, studying, or other creative pursuits.

Unless you're in prison and the warden controls your time, you'll need some structure that works for you, but the less rigid the better.

If any of these help, use them. If none of them do, that's the whole point of this book.

Dayparting

To borrow a media term, we can daypart our productivity as another option if you don't find time blocking beneficial. If you control your own schedule, whether you're a student, freelancer, work from home, or run your own business, dayparting is worth trying.

Divide your day into three or four parts, depending on your sleep schedule. One simple way is to divide by meals. Morning runs from breakfast to lunch, afternoon from lunch to dinner, evening from dinner to midnight, and night from midnight to breakfast. If you're a **biphasic sleeper** who also naps, divide it accordingly.

Tailor your tasks to the time of day when you're usually most focused. Instead of blocking out 9–10 a.m. for class reading, give those chapters a Morning part. As long as you get to them before lunch, you're on track. Instead of penciling in 1–2 p.m. for email, assign it to the Afternoon. It doesn't matter when you do it as long as it gets done before dinner.

Dayparting requires some mindfulness. What do you usually feel like doing in the mornings? What tasks are more tolerable in the afternoon? When are you most focused?

You won't always get it right. Do what you can and adjust as your day progresses. It's a guideline for your time, not a rigid rule.

Make It a Task Day

If dayparting doesn't work for you, go bigger and try Task Days. Task Days work best when you have full days at your disposal. If your schedule is largely your own, this gives you even more flexibility than dayparting.

Dedicate the entire day to a segment of your work. Schedule an all-day time slot if you anticipate interruptions or aren't entirely motivated to complete it. The more attention you give to a single topic, the greater the chance you'll find your focus and get more done.

Divide your days into the broad categories of your work. Design, websites, and projects on Monday. Writing on Tuesday. Social media on Wednesday. Admin on Thursday. Errands and chores on Friday. You may feel more focused early in the week for complex work and want to ease off toward the end. Switch days around as the week develops. The categories are yours to arrange.

If you're reading this book, you've already tried habits, routines, and discipline. You've tried time blocking, the Pomodoro Technique, tracking, and probably a dozen more I haven't mentioned. If they worked, you wouldn't be here. So ghost them. The energy you've been wasting trying to force habits that never stick could be used to get things done.

***

Quick Take

- Habits are optional. You can function without them.
- If habits, routines, and discipline have never stuck, stop forcing them.
- These are tools. Use them when they help, drop them when they don't.
- Ghost the advice that was never built for you.

Ghost Habit #4

Don't Plan to Plan

Trade Your To-Do List for a Task List

The worry with dropping habits and routines is that you'll end up paralyzed by decisions every morning. The **Task List** fixes that. You'll always know what to work on next without having to decide from scratch every morning.

There is hardly a productivity strategy that doesn't use a to-do list. It's generally the first go-to strategy for anyone looking to improve productivity.

It may be counterproductive. The name alone implies that anything less than full completion is a failure. We make our to-do lists with the intention that they will be the actions we take each day. As we complete them, we dutifully check the boxes next to each one.

By the time the day is done, when we're staring at a column of unchecked boxes on our to-do list, we've failed. We've set ourselves up by adding negativity to our already difficult effort to get things done.

I gave up on the to-do list years ago and now use a Task List, which is what I use throughout this book. Keeping a running list of what you need to do is one of the few things that consistently works for people like us.

Focus on the task, not its planning. The things we enjoy and do naturally don't need to go on the list. If you wake up and feel like going on a 10-mile hike or cleaning out your refrigerator, you'll do it.

The problem is the days we don't want to do things we don't like, like washing a month's worth of laundry or making a phone call to someone we don't know. We need to prompt ourselves to get them done.

If you can easily motivate yourself to load and run your dishwasher regularly, that doesn't go on your list. But if two or three days go by and you still can't face the ever-increasing pile of dirty dishes in your sink, that is a task you need to tackle immediately. Write it on your Task List. Writing it down on paper elevates its importance and makes it harder to ignore.

Create Your Task List

Your Task List should be very basic. One sheet of paper is all you need. Fold the paper in half twice, and you've got four boxes.

Now label the top of each quadrant.

Box 1–Top Left: **Now**

Box 2–Top Right: **Later**

Box 3–Bottom Left: **Everyday**

Box 4–Bottom Right: **Remember**

NOW	LATER
Make dentist appointment Call the landlord about the broken door Clean out fridge	Vacuum all the floors Return library books on Monday Oil change due in 3 days
EVERYDAY	**REMEMBER**
Take vitamins Bring headphones Stretch for 5 minutes Eat a snack at 2 p.m.	Cancel streaming subscription in 10 days Billie's birthday on the 15th Renew driver's license next month

Write the date at the top of the page and add only the things you need to do. Adding things you think you might want to do will only muddy your list and pull you away from the essentials.

Now is for tasks you want to complete as soon as possible, meaning by the end of your day or at the latest, the next day.

Later is for tasks or projects you'll presumably get to soon, ideally within the next few days. You can move to this list if you complete the Now box.

Everyday is for tasks like remembering to take vitamins, checking your mailbox, and drinking water. It's for critical daily actions you're likely to forget. These come back every day. Cross them off, but they'll be there again tomorrow until they no longer apply.

Remember is for important future events you want to keep fresh in your mind, like an upcoming appointment, remembering to cancel a trial subscription, a friend's birthday, or anything else that isn't immediate but you're worried you'll forget.

To get started, write down three immediate tasks you need to do, ones you need some prompting to remember. Three is the limit. More than that and you're back to the problem you started with.

The Task List is simpler than anything you've tried before. No analyzing urgency versus importance, no mental gymnastics, no color-coding. You're not categorizing by importance. You're only organizing by when you need to think about it. The **Eisenhower Matrix** is for people whose brains can manage that level of decision-making. This is for people whose brains can't.

You're not going to organize your extensive Lego collection before you mow your backyard, which looks like it's well on its way to becoming a jungle scene in *Predator*. Your priority for that day is the yard work.

This list is helpful to keep yourself on track. People tend to remember better what they write out by hand. You don't know when you'll finish it. It's a running list, and if you can't focus on a task, you can return to it later. Out of sight, out of mind. If it's in front of you, you'll have no choice but to see it.

Whatever tasks you don't finish today, you'll get to tomorrow or during your next work session. If something has been there a long time and you haven't gotten to it, lose it. You know you. Consider taking it off the list if it's not required. Cross out the date and use the same list if you choose.

We can't predict our mood in three days or what tasks we'll be able to focus on, but we can write down things we absolutely have to remember. Your Task List is only for the important tasks you need to remember to do, not a place for tasks you might want to do someday.

Out of Sight, Out of Mind

When your mind is scattered, you quickly lose track of what you should be doing.

Sometimes it's not that you are actively trying to avoid a task. The task is not on your mind when you might be most inclined to do it. You won't remember it if it's outside your immediate field of vision.

Keep your Task List and notes you'll need in front of you. Set reminders on your phone for tasks, events, or appointments you won't remember. Set reminders on multiple devices if you're severely time blind and won't check your primary device. Use alarms as reminders to get back to work, to take a break, or to check your email.

The goal is to eventually recognize those cues on your own without relying on technology to prompt you. But if you need the reminders permanently, use them permanently. There's no shame in that.

The ideal is to complete the task as soon as you receive it or when you become aware of it. Short of that, reminders like a Task List help. Ideally, if you do them immediately, they won't end up on your Task List.

Tasks I'm thinking about are more likely to get done if I'm reminded every day or a few times a day. If I write them down and keep that list in a place where I spend most of my time, like my desk or whiteboard,

I can't avoid seeing it. I'll have a better chance of completing them because they constantly refresh my mind.

I keep a notebook with a list of my goals in it. I don't look at it every day or every week, maybe a few times a year. Goals are removed, and goals are added. The greatest value of the list is that it brings these ideas back into my mind. They are spinning in the background even when I'm not conscious of it.

Too Many Choices, Zero Progress

Sometimes, you don't have a choice about how many tasks you have. Sometimes you do, and you take on too much. You overestimate what you can accomplish and what you'll have the mental energy to do. In addition, for many of us neurodivergent folks, it's difficult to estimate how long a task will take.

We can't focus well when we have several projects swirling around. We need to devote all our energy and attention to the most pressing tasks at hand. People with executive dysfunction are overwhelmed by the number of tasks and which to begin first.

If you have many important projects, you first have to decide which one to start with.

You write down a list of ten important tasks you want to do today. You begin with Task #1, but you might have done a better job on Task #4 if only you'd started with that one. You might skip around the list. The entire time you're working on Task #7, you think you should have been doing #3. Maybe you could have completed Task #9 relatively quickly if you'd chosen it first.

With too many options, you're thinking about doing something else, no matter which one you choose. It's always possible the other one would be more interesting, more enjoyable, easier to get going on. So you second-guess every choice before you've even started.

When you have too many tasks and projects going on at once, you can't focus properly on any of them. That affects the quality of the work you're putting in. You won't get much done, and what you do produce won't be your best effort.

Monotask, Don't Multitask

You're kidding yourself if you think you can successfully juggle several projects simultaneously. We may also be the "yes" types who take on commitments when we should instead limit the number of tasks we take on.

Keep three tasks available, but focus on only one at a time. I never know which one I'll be inclined to do on a given day. My mood, the time of day, what's going on in the house, how I slept, what I just read, any of it can make a task feel doable or impossible, but usually for the worse. Having a few options means I can pick whichever one I can get moving on instead of staring at the one thing that isn't happening.

When you choose a task, stick to it until you finish or you can no longer focus. Switching between tasks can pull you away from your original motivation and make it difficult to return to it.

As neurodivergent individuals, we likely have trouble transitioning between tasks. In many cases, monotasking comes more naturally to someone who hyperfocuses. Have a few tasks or activities on standby if you can no longer continue with the primary objective. Do something that keeps your synapses firing but gives you a break from the task that's wearing you down.

Three tasks on the list mean three choices, not 30. That's enough to get started without the paralysis.

Prioritize Your Task List

Your first step to prioritizing your Task List is to think about all your tasks, from daily to urgent, upcoming to those that are almost completed but still need attention. You can shrink the list from there.

Next week, you have a dentist appointment to make, five chapters to read in your textbook, a cable bill due on Friday, a trip to the grocery store on

Monday, a prescription to pick up, an oil change for your car, a text to your landlord about the leaky faucet, and hiring a graphic designer for a project.

Consider what's most time-critical, what you can delegate, what can wait, and what could become a bigger problem if you wait too long.

Which tasks will you forget to do if you're not prompted? That's what needs to go on your Task List. For instance, you do your shopping on your day off, Monday, so that doesn't need to go on your list.

Make your tasks specific and give them a deadline if they're imminent. Don't write, "Pay bills." If your cell phone bill is due on Thursday, write down that you need to pay it by Wednesday. Don't wait until the last second when something could go wrong. Pay it before the due date to give yourself an extra buffer.

Identify which tasks you need to do first. Don't assign too many each day. Match your mood and focus level as much as possible.

Only take on what you can reasonably complete without exhausting yourself. That makes it easier for you later on. You ultimately choose what you can handle in the moment. That's how this works.

Glance at your list throughout the week. You can keep using the same sheet for several days if not much changes. When it gets cluttered or out of date, start a fresh one and carry over whatever you didn't finish.

This doesn't mean you have to do them in the order you wrote them. You'll do what you can do when you can do it. But knowing what's most important helps you make better choices when you're deciding what to tackle.

How to Pick Without Freezing

There are a few schools of thought here. Do the easiest tasks or the ones you can quickly finish first. Do the most demanding tasks first. Do the tasks you feel most like doing first.

Many choose to start with the simplest tasks. Completing the easiest ones first incentivizes them to take on the bigger tasks.

I start with the ones I'm most in the mood to do. If you're thinking about them and want to do them, you're more likely to continue with your immediate or long-term tasks. Accomplishing something early gets the day rolling.

Others like to knock out the most challenging tasks first so they can coast through the rest as their motivation wanes. I don't often have the focus needed for that at the start of my day, even with a full pot of coffee.

What This Looks Like Day-to-Day

It's Monday morning. You've got three things in your Now box. Email the client back, buy groceries, and pay the electric bill.

The most important? The email. The most urgent? The electric bill. The easiest? Also, the electric bill. You're barely functioning.

You could follow the "do the most important first" rule and tackle the email. But your brain isn't willing right now, so you don't. You pay the electric bill instead because it's easy and you can manage it. One thing done.

You look at the list again. Email or groceries? Both feel impossible right this minute.

So you check your Everyday box. Walk for 30 minutes. Take out the trash. Empty the dishwasher. Refill your water bottle. You can do these. Four things done.

If it's noon and you can't go on, you did four things, and that's enough for now. If it's 2 p.m. and you've got energy, go back to Now. Maybe the email feels doable. Or maybe you go get groceries. Whichever you're capable of at that time.

There's no wrong choice here. Some days you'll start with the hardest task because you've got the energy for it. Some days you'll start with the easiest because that's all you've got. Some days you'll do the one you feel like doing most. Some days you'll do nothing from your Now list and just take out the trash.

This is what productivity looks like for people like us. You're not following a rigid order. You're picking what you can handle. That's what you can do.

The Task of Least Resistance

When you look at your Task List and freeze because you don't know which task to pick, use this tool.

Choose the task you're most motivated to do, given what conditions allow. Not the most important one, not the most urgent one, not the one you think you should do. The one you can make yourself do in this moment.

If you can't make yourself write an email, but you feel like doing laundry, do the laundry. You're moving, you're building momentum, and you're not paralyzed anymore.

Once you're moving, you might find energy for the harder tasks. You might not. Either way, you did something instead of nothing.

This might feel wrong. Productivity advice tells you to do the hardest thing first, to get the difficult task out of the way before your willpower runs out. That works when you've got the energy for it. When you don't, the **Task of Least Resistance** is what gets you off the couch.

Write Everything Down

Write it all down. Every idea, every solution that pops into your head, everything you want to remember. I mean those moments of brilliance you have, or those great thoughts you want to hold on to. This is separate from the daily activities we write on our Task List.

Trust me, you'll forget. And what happens when you forget? You'll spend extra time tracking down the information you lost, though that's not always possible. Sometimes, it's gone forever.

Whiteboard it, put it in your Notes, or write it on a sticky note. Take a screenshot or photo to remind you if you don't have time to write. Record a voice message and transcribe it later. Make sure you write legibly. Your notes are useless if you can't read them later.

I can swear I'll remember a website I heard on the radio. Thirty minutes later, I'm online, searching through radio ads. My mind is excellent at remembering the tiniest details of an obscure geographical location I learned in 6th grade, but I won't remember a person's name I heard 10 minutes ago.

Letting your mind work through problems in its own way is part of your neurodivergence. Our minds are constantly working through problems, seeking out solutions. If you think you can complete projects and reason through problems in your own way, make sure to document your solutions before they're lost to the next thought or anti-task on the horizon.

I can't commit a set amount of time to writing out a lengthy weekly schedule, but I can write notes as I go. The thought of maintaining a daily schedule is demoralizing. I'd be lucky to manage a handful of days.

I forget what I'm doing, just walking from room to room. My mind constantly whirls with concepts and ideas, especially in problem-solving mode. You'll have your "Look! Squirrel!" moments, where you'll see something shiny and completely forget what you were working on.

Write down your important thoughts as they come to you. It doesn't matter if you're standing in line at the post office, waiting to pick up your kids from school, or just about to close your eyes tucked in your bed. Many people do their best problem-solving just before falling asleep or in the shower. Write it down when it hits you, even at 2 a.m.

You'll swear you'll remember it in the morning, but that's highly unlikely. Don't wait. That insightful solution will disappear if you wait too long. You won't get it back, and if you remember some of it, it won't be in the same form as before.

A notes app on your phone is ideal for jotting down thoughts instantly. Without one, I'd lose half my writing and ideas. Look for one that can launch from the lock screen for quicker access.

A voice recorder app works well if you're more auditory or can't type because you're driving or in the shower. Yes, you can record notes in the shower.

Sometimes it helps to write down what tasks you've completed. If you vacuum your bedroom and study for an hour, write it down. Reviewing what you've done is inspiring for some and may give you that dopamine hit from seeing what you've accomplished.

If the information you need is there at your fingertips, you're more likely to use it. Most of us are lost without clear direction. We often need to be nudged into taking the necessary action. The tools we need should be easily accessible.

On Paper or in the Cloud?

I write down every idea, future plan, or potential solution that comes to mind.

I use small staple-bound notebooks to record my ideas as they come to me. They're lightweight and cheap enough to keep several around. One is next to my bed, another on my desk, and another I carry in my laptop bag. Pretty much a notebook within reach wherever I am.

An idea that popped into your head at 1 a.m. could be exactly what you need to complete your project. As much as I'd like to, I can't sit down for two hours and force that to happen.

It's important not to worry about how it looks. Get your thoughts down. If they're random thoughts with duplicate points written upside down, as long as you can decipher them later, it makes no difference.

You may not use most of what you write down. Even if you disregard 90% of what's on the papers, it's worth the 10% of thoughts you can use further.

If you'd rather write it in a notes app on your phone, that's equally good. If you go this route, a basic organization system helps you find things quickly.

There are an overwhelming number of note-taking apps available. Whatever you're looking for, basic or advanced features, free or paid, offline capability, or access across devices, you'll find one that fits. A current list of note-taking options is available at resources.ghosthabits.com.

Auditory thinkers can skip the typing and record notes with a voice-recording app installed on their phone. This requires more time to review and organize, but it's the best method to capture your ideas and important information on the fly.

The Dollar Store Notebook Works Fine

The old design principle holds. Keep it Simple, Stupid. You have enough to worry about in life. You don't need a complicated process to track your tasks.

Get the tools you want to use, the ones you'll look forward to using. But only make it as complicated as you'll reasonably use. Expensive supplies are overkill. Imported Japanese pencils or costly monthly subscriptions to time management apps are a waste of money unless they compel you to stay productive. A cheap dollar-store notebook might be just as useful for you.

It doesn't matter what you use as long as it keeps you going.

You need something to write with and something to write on. That's it. Low tech is fine. A notepad, whiteboard, index cards, sticky notes, or papyrus, if that's what you've got. Chalk, a quill pen, crayon, or a stylus will do the job.

The right tools will encourage you to be more productive. I'll admit I'm a borderline office supply hoarder. I almost exclusively write with bold roller gel pens. Anything else doesn't feel quite right. I prefer lines and grids on my paper, which should be thick enough so that no trace of the words on the opposite side is visible. That's particular, I know, but with ideal materials, I'll want to write more and keep better notes. Find what works for you.

Linear vs. Lateral Thinking

I'm impressed by people who can plan a project on paper. That stack of notebooks on my shelf sits largely untouched because I can't organize my thoughts into any legible structure.

You want to create an outline for a thesis or a story. It may be nearly impossible for you to plot the major sections in a clear numerical order. You hop around from concept to concept. As a result, the pages look like a mashup of unintelligible phrases with arrows pointing in every direction.

If you create a numbered list, you'll need to add more as you think of new ideas. That requires large gaps between topics or subheadings, which makes it look sloppy and hard to follow.

A beginning, middle, and end sequence doesn't work for you because you don't process information in a sequential order.

You may not be a linear thinker who can visualize the steps. Instead, your brain is lateral, making non-consecutive connections. You can still record the information on paper, but you don't get there in the same way.

Some people find that a strict planner of schedules, calendars, and deadlines keeps them focused and on task. Others insist that, in addition to their schedules, journaling their thoughts and reflections, brainstorming, or tracking goals and habits improves their productivity. I marvel at people who can write out their plans and goals on paper with consistent, legible handwriting in straight, clean lines.

If you're not one of them, you might have to write the pages again and again. My journal attempts are full of crossed-out words and sections, with additional notes added throughout.

But don't let your perfectionism get in the way. I didn't want my journals to look messy, so I'd write my lists on paper first, then copy them into the "real" journal. You can imagine how much time I wasted trying to make it neat.

If you truly enjoyed journaling, you wouldn't need habit trackers or charts to guilt yourself into doing it.

Organizing Your Task List

Once you've created your Task List, you'll need to keep it up. But don't overthink this either.

Some days your Task List will be neat. Some days it'll be messy with things crossed out and scribbled in the margins. Either is fine.

Rewrite it when it's too messy to read or when you've crossed off most tasks and need a fresh start. Leave it when rewriting it feels like more work than it's worth. Spending 20 minutes making a clean new list when the old one was still readable is the kind of thing that drains energy when you could have spent that on a task.

The point is to have your tasks visible. Cross things out. Write new things in margins. Use the same sheet for three days if it's still working. When the list stops working because it's too chaotic, that's the time to rewrite it.

If You Can't Find It, You Won't Use It

Now you've gotten your thoughts down on paper, on your phone, or in a document file, but they're in disarray.

Keep your notes and Task List accessible. If it's in front of you, you'll see it and use it. Taking meticulous notes is pointless if you never review them, so try to stick to a day, time, or occasion to review, like first thing in the morning, on the train to work, every Sunday night, or a few minutes here and there when you think of it.

Digital notes are easier to revise and edit. Save only what you need so you don't have to continually reread old, unimportant notes.

If you're taking your notes on paper, you've got to review them more often to prevent another pile of papers to deal with. If you're scribbling on sticky notes, rewrite important info in a semi-permanent place and toss the sticky notes. If you're reviewing notebook pages, cross out anything outdated or unimportant. If something's indispensable, write it again in that semi-permanent place.

Your long-term goals are different from your daily Task List. Our future goals take longer to accomplish, so writing them down in one place is a good practice. We'll have them for reference and periodic review, which can revive your interest in the ones you want to pick up again someday. After all, you wrote them down for a reason.

My long-term and future goals are still written in an old, worn, plastic-covered notebook I've had for almost a decade. Fortunately, I recognized my extreme disorganization and chose a refillable notebook so I could easily add, rearrange, or remove pages.

This sad-looking thing has seen years of lists and notes from my ever-changing goals, travel plans, phone numbers, email addresses, expenses, doctor's appointments, account numbers, and even the trials and tribulations of selling my house. It's a hodgepodge of information scribbled on random pages. Yet I still refer to it when I need to check an old name or number.

When I bought this notebook, I knew my thoughts were scattered, and keeping all my important information in one place, even if it was disorganized, was the best option. Like many with ADHD, I know exactly where to find the information I need amongst the disheveled pages.

If things go off the rails and I fall back into my old ways, I'd return to this all-in-one approach in a heartbeat. It kept me functional for many years.

You can also take this flexible approach. My notebook fulfilled the basic need of having all my important information in one place. That may work for you if you're as disorganized as I am, but you can still make some sense of the chaos.

Another option is to create a single physical location, like a desk drawer, a file folder, or a large container, to store your most important personal information. This prevents you from wasting time searching through stacks of paper or flipping through random notebooks when you need to find a document immediately.

You can also keep all your information in online files, though if you're concerned with security or data loss, this may not be your best option. Encrypt and back up your files regularly, especially if they contain highly confidential information you wouldn't want to get out.

Try a Brain Dump

Organizing my thoughts coherently is a formidable part of any project. I have a hard time deciding what to do and in what order.

Frequently, our thoughts are so mixed up that we can't assemble them into a usable order. A brain dump is a quick freewriting session that allows you to record all your thoughts, feelings, and ideas.

In this exercise, write down everything you're thinking, completely unfiltered.

Write down anything that comes to mind. Fresh ideas. New goals. Future plans. Your current state of mind. Potential projects. Worries you have.

You can also do a strictly work-related brain dump, limiting your writing to new business ideas or creative solutions for work problems that need solving.

A brain dump is much like a screenshot of your thoughts at any given time. What you're thinking about today won't be exactly what you're thinking tomorrow.

When you've got it all down on paper, review your writing session. There, we can discern what's bothering us, what's holding us back, and often where the problem lies.

Taking everything out of your head and putting it down on paper lets you see the bigger picture. Sometimes we get stuck on the details and can't see how to put it together until we can see it in its entirety, right in front of us. The nonlinear way your mind works is what a brain dump is designed for.

ADHD brains in particular tend toward divergent thinking. More ideas, more unexpected connections, more originality. A brain dump is designed for exactly that kind of mind, which is why getting everything out of your head and onto paper reveals more than you realized was in there.

Mind mapping can be another valuable tool for organizing your thoughts and ideas, digitally, on paper, or on a whiteboard. Begin with a central thought, then create bubbles of connected ideas that branch outward from it. This process helps give your thoughts a sense of order, allowing you to build on them.

Both methods can help you organize the chaos you feel when your thoughts overwhelm you.

Accountability Buddy

Sometimes it's enough to know someone else knows your tasks and expects you to do them. That real or imagined obligation is sometimes all it takes.

Body doubling and accountability work differently. Body doubling is the presence of having someone nearby while you work, even if they're doing something unrelated. Accountability is an obligation, knowing someone expects you to finish the task. Some people respond to one and not the other. Try both and see which one your brain uses.

For accountability, you can work with a friend, family member, or coworker who knows what you're trying to accomplish and expects you to follow through. If other people rely on you to do your part, you face a bigger consequence, increasing the chance you'll apply yourself and do it. You don't want to be "that guy," and I use that in a gender-neutral sense, who deprives their buddy of their reward after they worked so hard to do their share.

For those who don't have a human accountability buddy, being accountable to a pet can work for some people. Tell Mr. Wiggles you'll sit at your desk and fill out those time sheets until they're logged, and then follow through.

For body doubling, several apps offer virtual options. You switch on your video camera, share your goals, and work remotely with a stranger for a set period. Seeing another person diligently working can motivate you to complete your tasks. If you can't arrange an online meeting time or prefer not to be on camera, some apps let you coordinate to finish the task off-camera by the end of the day.

It's only useful if others' approval drives you. If you don't care that someone else is working simultaneously or that someone expects results, you have nothing invested in whether you procrastinate. Having your Task List in front of you serves the same purpose at zero social cost.

Suffer Now or Suffer Later...But Worse

Most people, many neurotypicals included, tend to put off things they don't want to do or feel they may not do successfully. Another group tempts fate and puts it off until the very last minute.

You delay renewing your driver's license because it's too much trouble or you don't want to take a new photo, so you tempt fate by driving around with an expired license. You delay sending an email where you need to regrettably tell the recipient no because you don't want to hurt their feelings. You don't pay attention to your credit card's due date, which puts you at risk of paying the bill late and getting hit with an outrageously high fee.

When I was in college, I took that to an extreme. I delayed taking an introductory calculus course until my final semester. I'd never call myself a math person. At the time, I struggled with being away from home for the first time and finding my place in college life. I didn't want to compound my stress by taking a class I had no aptitude for, though I knew it was mandatory to graduate.

This wasn't my finest idea, and I was even more stressed after fulfilling all the other degree requirements. My entire college diploma came down to this one class I did not want to take. Because I waited, I had to take costly additional electives to remain a full-time student and work night shifts as a grocery store stocker to pay off a small portion of the extra tuition.

As a result, I barely passed the class, and it taught me that putting things off may seem tolerable for a time, but it's not good in the long run. I could have taken the calculus course in my sophomore year when my workload was lighter, and I didn't have to work overnight shifts and then rush off to class half-asleep, but I didn't want the stress at that time.

Part of prolonging the dread is knowing you'll eventually have to do it, but it doesn't need immediate attention. As an overthinker, it never escaped my mind. With every semester, the anxiety built as the clock ran out. Some nights, I felt like a condemned prisoner when I'd run my mental calculator and lie awake, thinking about how much time I had left.

To graduate, I had to take out additional student loans I hadn't planned on. Procrastination can be expensive, and that side effect impacted me for decades after graduation.

The Deadline Problem

The world runs on deadlines. We may think of the old-school journalist in a frantic newsroom, pencil behind the ear, feverishly typing out the story to get it to press in time. But throughout our lives, we constantly attempt to meet our deadlines, hard deadlines like tax filing, final exams, or weddings, and other, more flexible, soft deadlines, like doing a home renovation project, scheduling a routine checkup, or planning a trip. Their scale of impact on our lives ranges from annoyance to full-blown panic.

If you guessed that the word "deadline" has a grim origin, you're right. It dates back to Civil War military prisons, where a line was marked around the perimeter that prisoners weren't allowed to cross.

Guards were ordered to shoot anyone who touched it. The dead line. Lucky for us, over the decades it softened to mean a time limit.

What's the difference between that scenario and how we currently struggle to focus on our tasks when we don't have a reason to begin the task immediately, even though we know it must be done eventually?

It would be easier if internal deadlines worked, meaning those we impose on ourselves. If you set a deadline of 3 p.m. tomorrow to file or shred all the junk mail accumulated on your dining room table, what are the chances you'll do it?

If you were given an entire week to complete a task but could say to yourself, "I want to complete this task before lunch today," and then you actually did it, you could apply that to everything on your list. Your productivity would skyrocket, and your stress and anxiety over it would plunge. But in this reality, unless you're motivated to do it, there's almost zero chance you will.

What would motivate you to do it right away? Perhaps you're obsessed with that activity, you're doing it as a favor for someone else, it will benefit your future, you'd get recognition for it, or you'd make money.

If none of these apply and there's no other advantage for you, what then?

You probably don't do it. If you really don't want to or find it too difficult, and there is no imminent deadline to do it, it'll probably get set aside indefinitely unless or until circumstances change. If you've been dealing with this cycle for years, you know how it works. No amount of telling yourself to get it done right this minute spurs you into action.

The difference comes when external deadlines are imposed on us.

Of course, if you're given two weeks to complete a work project, an external deadline with a negative consequence that you didn't choose, it would be ideal to start on it immediately and get it done. That will give you time to research, consult, edit, write, proofread, double-check, and triple-check. But unless you're completely motivated and thinking about this project constantly, it will most likely be put on the back burner for a while.

You don't see the project as an immediate fire to put out. We respond exceptionally well to situations we consider a crisis, but we don't classify everyday tasks as a crisis, they sit in the back of our minds as things we'll get to eventually. It gets priority on our internal task list only when the situation changes, and it's a "do it now or face drastic negative consequences" situation.

You're assigned a term paper for your Monday morning class, due in a month. Fantastic. One whole month to write a paper.

However, if you arrive at class on Wednesday morning and your instructor explains, "Sorry, change of plans. I need those papers turned in by next Wednesday." That new bit of information changes everything. If not submitting it on time means you fail, which tanks your grade in the class, which results in a lower overall GPA, a possible loss of scholarship, and a lower chance of getting into your first-choice graduate program, you'll find the motivation to start on it ASAP. You would never have done that if you had three more weeks to finish.

You found your motivation. Or your motivation, in the form of a deadline, was provided for you.

The reasons that motivate us to do things we don't want to do, such as financial cost, guilt, others' disappointment, shame, or loss of status or power, differ from person to person. Still, they have one thing in common. They have consequences that we desperately want to avoid.

The No-Deadline Trap

Our imposed work schedules tend to dictate what we have to do and when. If you work for an employer, consequences are built into the job. Someone else keeps us accountable for getting the work done.

Outside of work or school, our time is mostly our own. There aren't as many hard-and-fast deadlines or consequences. Of course, there are some obvious ones.

Don't pay your rent on time, get evicted.

Ignore the speed limit, incur costly fines.

Fail to pay those fines by the due date, lose your driver's license.

Pay your electric bill late, and it's candlelight, cold showers, take-out meals.

Neglect to turn down your death metal music at 2 a.m., get an unwanted and extremely aggressive knock on the door.

But if you're self-employed, or would like to be, or want to do side gigs to make money, you have total control over how to structure your time. Your deadlines are up to you to set and enforce. They aren't the same concrete deadlines with defined consequences for employment or education.

No one is holding your feet to the fire every day to complete your tasks. It's all on you to set your hours, do the paperwork, and get the job done.

These are exactly the tasks where the standard productivity advice fails you.

A Tool, Not a Habit

You're keeping a tool available for when you need it, not building a daily habit of checking your Task List.

Some days you'll be stuck and need to look at your list to figure out what to do next. On other days, you'll know exactly what needs to be done without reminders. Some weeks, the Task List will help you every single day. Other weeks, you won't think about it at all because you're functioning fine without it.

If checking your Task List every morning comes naturally to you, keep doing it. But if you have to force yourself to remember, if you're setting alarms or tracking how many days in a row you've used it, you're adding pressure that shouldn't be there.

Think of it like a hammer. You use a hammer when you need to hang a picture on the wall. When you're done, you put it back in the toolbox. Sometimes you don't need a hammer for weeks or months. The hammer still works perfectly fine the next time you need it.

The Task List works the same way. It's there when you're stuck and need help figuring out where to start. When you know what to do without checking it, you don't need to look at it.

Don't screw this up by trying to turn it into a habit. That defeats the entire purpose of **Ghost Habits**. There is no failure in forgetting the Task List exists for a while.

This Shouldn't Drain You

If creating or using your Task List feels exhausting, you're doing too much. It should only take a few minutes to write three things, and you're done. If you're spending twenty minutes on it, reorganizing and rewriting, you've made it too complicated. If planning your Task List feels hard, that's the sign you've gone too far.

One sheet of paper, four boxes. Write three things in the Now box that you've been putting off. Don't overthink it.

If you can't focus enough to make the list right now, skip it and just do one small thing. The list can wait. This is supposed to be easier than whatever you were doing before.

***

Quick Take

- One sheet of paper, four boxes: Now, Later, Everyday, Remember.
- The Now box holds up to three tasks. Do these today if you can.
- When stuck, choose the Task of Least Resistance.
- Write everything down. Your brain isn't storage.
- Deadlines already exist. Let them do the work.

Ghost Habit #5

Do What You Can When You Can

What Is Being Productive?

You've got your **Task List**. You know what needs doing. The problem is getting from knowing to doing when your energy is unpredictable, and your motivation doesn't run on a schedule.

Being productive is a big question to define. It means finishing things that need doing, at whatever pace you can manage, without running yourself into the ground. You're not going full force, charging through your workday and night. That's how you burn out in a week. We can't give it our maximum effort if we're not rested and ready.

If you think of it as a video game, keep the health bar as close to 100% as possible. You can't take on the boss at 30%, so don't start your days without rest or energy. But unlike a video game, you don't get instantly regenerated when you fail. You can correct mistakes, but it's not a magic do-over with zero consequences.

It requires taking care of yourself. Sleep, food, exercise, and medical care. Don't run on empty and expect to get anything done. Recharge by stepping away from your tasks and doing whatever helps you relax.

Start Small or Go Big

Start small, break everything into tiny steps. That can work, but it's not always good advice. Sometimes, starting small can make it harder to stay motivated. Sometimes you need to go big to get fired up about your project.

I want to join a gym to get back my six-pack abs. I can break this task into many small steps. Today, I'll make a list of gyms in my area. Tomorrow, I can review the websites and compare classes and facilities. I'll narrow down the options and compare membership plans the next day. The day after, I can choose a couple of gyms to check out.

Or you can skip straight to it. Today, I'll review my local gym websites and social media pages and schedule visits to a few. If you know you're ready to focus now but think you might lose motivation, there's more pain in dragging it out.

Several years ago, I had to have all four wisdom teeth pulled out. The very expensive oral surgeon gave me the option of pulling two teeth, allowing time to heal, and then returning the next month to have the other two pulled. No thanks, Doc. The pain and infection risk would persist much longer than if they were all pulled the same day. Who knows how much longer I would have delayed the second appointment if the first visit hadn't gone well?

As this unpleasant situation illustrates, there is less distress and a lower chance of procrastination when you tackle your tasks all at once.

Choose a Place to Begin

When you're facing a huge, overwhelming project, the hardest part is to figure out where to start.

Break it down to three levels. Choose a project, then choose a task within that project, then choose a starting point within that task.

Filing your income taxes becomes gathering your W-2s, which becomes going online to download your forms. Landscaping your yard becomes planting new trees and shrubs, which becomes measuring the area you need to plant.

The best place to start is wherever you believe the beginning is. If that's not doable, choose a place that will sustain your motivation, especially for tasks that don't need to be completed sequentially.

Most experts say the first step in building a website is getting a domain name and web hosting. That's fine, but it's not required. You can design the architecture on paper, start writing content, or research SEO. Start wherever you feel most inspired. Even within a single task, you can start anywhere. You can write website content in any order. It's up to you.

It's better to choose the wrong place to begin than not to start at all. There are few things in life you only get one attempt at. You can always fix it later, toss it out and start over, or discover you're not as fascinated with it as you thought. Discovering what we don't want is just as important as knowing what we do want.

Error: Instructions Unclear

I was once asked to create a banner for a non-profit community project. I stressed over this project for three weeks, so I went all in and made an extra-large, multicolored banner.

My mistake was not asking enough questions when first approached to do the project. I was too embarrassed to ask questions and assumed that others would instinctively know what was expected based on the information provided. I caused myself weeks of anxiety over this. As it turned out, my guess at what they were looking for was in the ballpark, but I made it much more complicated than needed.

Ultimately, my banner, the one I spent too much time and energy on, was shelved. Instead, the committee opted for a simple two-color, one-line banner that looked nothing like mine.

That's how it goes for a lot of us. When we don't know what's expected of us, we agonize about it and either go overboard or stall on completing the task because we don't know which direction to take.

If you're doing work for someone else, ask what's expected before you start. If it's your own project, define it for yourself first. Scope, skill level, deadline, required elements, and what a finished version looks like. Get those answers upfront and you won't spend three weeks like I did, working on the wrong thing.

When You Already Know What's Coming

You know exactly what the task is and you've done it before. You know how long it's going to take and how it feels halfway through, and you've already decided you don't want to do it before you've done a single thing. Knowing exactly what's coming doesn't make starting easier. Sometimes it makes it harder.

I've moved well over a dozen times in my life. Not small moves. Entire houses with moving trucks. I know how to do it. I know how long it takes, how my back feels after moving the furniture, when boxes get too heavy, and which room takes longer than expected. I've done it enough times that I could pack a kitchen in my sleep.

And when I needed to, I still couldn't make myself start.

The worst was the last time I sold my home and moved across the country. I'd been packing sporadically for weeks. But as the move date got closer, the paralysis set in. The moving truck was already there. The movers were carrying boxes out the door while I was still filling them. I packed right alongside them until the last possible minute. Whatever was left, I'd have to stuff into the car. I sprained my shoulder somewhere in there but I got it done.

When you need to do a time critical task like this, start as early as you can. Give yourself as much leeway as possible and you're less likely to hit a wall. But if you do, give it an honest try without setting a timer or an alarm. Start the task and go as long as you can, and you'll naturally check the clock when your brain starts pushing back. If you've gained some momentum by then, keep going, but if you haven't, stop there and don't try to force it past that point.

If that's where you stop, do whatever it takes to reset. A walk, music, something that takes your full attention for a while. Go do that, because feeling bad about not doing the task is the real danger. The frustration starts to feel worse than the task itself. Once your emotions are working against you, it takes longer to get out of that place than it would have taken to do the task.

The task isn't going anywhere. Your ability to start again is what's at risk if you stay in that spiral. Go reset and come back when you're ready. If it has to get done regardless of how you feel, the Hard Start Principle is coming up later in this chapter.

When Someone Puts a Clock on You

Your boss needs you to write an important email in fifteen minutes or your teacher just announced an in-class essay. Someone is standing there asking you a question about something you know all about and they want an answer now.

On a normal day you could write that email in ten minutes or answer that question without blinking. But the moment someone puts a clock on it, everything changes. The deadline that helps other people focus is the thing that shuts you down. And unlike most paralysis, you can't walk away and come back to this one. The clock is running whether you're able to do it or not.

The worst thing you can do is freeze completely. Clear your head as fast as you can. Take a breath. Focus on what you already know rather than what you don't. You weren't prepared for this, and that's not your fault, but you need to keep going. Do what you can without panicking. A panicked answer is worse than a slow one.

When Nothing on the List Sounds Possible

Sometimes you might feel inspired but don't feel like touching your Task List. The advice is to just do two minutes on a task you're not into. In my world, that doesn't work. It may be a mere two minutes for someone without time blindness, but for me, it may as well be two hours of the most uninteresting task imaginable. The thought that it's only a couple of minutes doesn't make it any more enticing.

I have to try a different route. If you find it challenging to focus on an uninteresting task, start with something you want to do.

Your job for the day is to work through the Task List as much as you can. If you clear everything in Now, that's a great day. Most days you won't, and that's fine. If you can't get started on anything in Now, move to something else productive and come back. Anticipate something you'll need to do soon or might add to your Task List later.

Say I have three tasks on my list today. Book flights for my summer vacation, refill my medication, and update monthly business records.

If none of those seem appealing and I don't feel like talking on the phone or researching online, then I have to find an alternative, productive task. I move on to my Later list. If nothing there seems doable either, then I need to find another productive task to do.

I know I'll need to do laundry in a day or two, so I'll get started and get it out of the way. It's not on my list, but it will be, and now it won't have to be.

Doing something useful, like sorting through the mail that's been piling up or scheduling an appointment you've been putting off, is a better use of your time when you feel inspired.

Once you've done the laundry or as it's washing, you might feel inspired to tackle other tasks. It's easier to keep going once you're in motion.

It took me two months to call and cancel an unused credit card.

I didn't know how long I'd be on hold. Ten minutes or two hours? The uncertainty was a huge factor. I could be doing something more enjoyable. For someone who despises phone calls, anything is more enjoyable. I didn't want to think about credit cards. Talking about finances reminds me of times when I was in serious debt, and it ruins my mood.

I hesitated because I didn't know what to say. What if they pushed back? I wrote down all the info I thought I'd need so I could read it if my mind went blank. If you have absolutely no idea what to say, an AI assistant can write you a draft for a phone call or email. Give it the situation and ask for a script.

It was a simple task. But I didn't do it until it potentially affected my credit score. As it turned out, the phone call was brief, lasting only a few minutes.

After that, I felt relieved to finally get it off my mind and used that motivation to tackle more tasks. I wasted more time and energy avoiding the task than I would have spent just doing it.

Whatever it is in life, it's usually not as bad as we think. We prove this repeatedly, but each time a difficult task arises, we fall into the same thinking and put it off, creating a bigger obstacle.

When you finish one task, use that momentum to start the next. Think of it like the debt snowball method. Your monthly payment goes to a small debt, and when that's paid off, you roll that same payment to the next debt, then the next, paying off all your debts in less time.

When you start with a task you're motivated to do, use the momentum from that success to complete the next on your Task List. Small wins build on each other the same way.

Use Your Time Bites

A **time bite** is any small fraction of time you can actually use, even a few free minutes.

Whenever I travel, especially by train or plane, I tend to wildly overestimate how much work or studying I can get done. I'll copy files to my tablet, thinking I'll do three or four hours of uninterrupted work. That doesn't happen. Instead, I'm dozing off or half-engaged with the latest indie drama on my tiny screen.

I usually manage to get some work done, even if it's only mapping out solutions to problems. Tuning out my surroundings gives me uninterrupted time to think.

The same applies to shorter moments, like when you're waiting for a phone or video call to begin, the endless ads before a YouTube video, your cup of tea to brew, the washer to finish its last spin, the bus to arrive, or for someone to pick you up.

When you realize you have nothing pressing, throw yourself into a task. Sometimes, the inspiration to write down ideas or compose an email may be fleeting, only seconds before you lose it. Many of my long-term projects began with short bursts of downtime, like waiting for a meeting to start or standing in line.

In that short time bite, you can do something useful to make your life easier later. Clear your desk so you can actually find things. Do a quick lesson on your phone. Review your Task List and see if anything feels doable soon. Scribble down notes for a project before the idea disappears. Load the dishes that have been sitting in the sink. Return the email you've been putting off for a week. Change your bedding before you forget again.

You've already committed your future time. Use the minutes you have now.

Automate Everything You Can

Automating whatever you can is one way to get tasks off your list before they even get there. Set up auto-pay on recurring bills. Put prescription refills on automatic. Use reminders and alarms for anything you'll forget, like appointments, medications, and the things that turn into bigger problems when you forget them. Filter your email so the junk doesn't clog up your inbox. These things take time to set up once, and then they're done.

I've had auto-pay on most of my bills for years. I set it for the minimum payment, which gives me the option to pay more if I have the funds.

If your financial situation allows for it, outsourcing more, cleaning, grocery delivery, laundry, prepared meals, whatever you don't have the energy for, is worth it when you can swing it.

Do It When You See It

When trying to keep our lives as organized as possible, the best policy is always to do our tasks as soon as we get them. That's especially important when it comes to our household chores. If we let things go, before we know it, we can end up with a cluttered, messy home that requires a commercial dumpster, a team of professional cleaners, and, quite possibly, a TV crew.

This is another instance of when the question, "What is the best decision I can make right now?" comes into play. If you do it now when you're thinking of it, you won't have to do it later.

Curb time spent on future tasks by following a few basic rules like:

Put items away that you're no longer using in the room where they belong.

Put your dirty dishes in the dishwasher after eating and clean up messes as you make them.

Have a dedicated place to hang up your coat, set your shoes, and leave your phone and keys.

Sort through letters and papers immediately, and put unneeded papers in the recycling box.

Fold and put away laundry as you take it out of the dryer.

If it's not essential, trash it now instead of later.

None of these are complicated. The hard part is remembering to do them when your brain is already thinking about so many other things.

Give Junebugging a Go

Even so, you may find that your cleaning skills aren't up to par, or you don't know where to start.

One way to get more done, especially household chores, is to adopt a method called **Junebugging**.

Junebugging is a method that came out of the ADHD community around 2020 and spread through Reddit and TikTok. It got its name from a beetle that always returns to the same location. It's well-suited for fidgety ADHD folks who need to get up and move.

You set your location, let's say your bathroom, and begin your task there. You spray down the shower doors and scrub the walls. As you're doing that, you notice the wastebasket is overflowing. You empty it, and on your way, you see the kitchen trash is also full. You take all the trash outside and return to the bathroom. The towels need changing. You head for the linen closet and walk past the stack of newspapers on your kitchen table. You drop them in the recycle bin, grab the towels, and return to the bathroom.

You see where this is going. You always return to the original location until all tasks in that location are completed, no matter how often you get distracted by other tasks.

If you're still motivated to clean after finishing all the tasks in that location, choose a new one and start over.

You may not get to every task you intend to do and may also do additional tasks that you didn't anticipate doing that day. Either way, you are completing tasks that eventually need to be done, which is a major boost to your productivity.

We can broadly apply it to tasks beyond cleaning. Choose a home base, a spot you keep coming back to, and return to it throughout the workday until the tasks there are done. For instance, you can set your email inbox as your location. Despite whatever else you get distracted doing, you'll always return to reading, sorting, or trashing emails until it's completely cleared out.

Do One, Get One Free

Another option for low-focus tasks is task pairing to get two things done at once. Think about what additional complementary task you can do right now, along with the task you're already doing. Monotasking is the best strategy for highly focused tasks that need your full attention, but when doing something that requires little focus, find something else to add to it.

For instance, fold laundry while watching a movie, type your shopping list while standing in line at the DMV, get on your stationary bike during a phone call, sweep the floor while your lunch heats in the microwave.

When I'm on phone calls, I clean. Not running the vacuum or starting the dishwasher, but sweeping, dusting, and especially going from room to room putting things back in their place. I'm getting things done, and the person on the other end is none the wiser. Sometimes I look forward to calls because I can do the cleaning I normally can't force myself to do, since my mind is focused on the caller.

Being in the neurodivergent world means we're not always able to harness our focus when needed. It's another way to pay it forward to ourselves when we can tack on one or more tasks when they're least unpleasant for us to do, saving ourselves aggravation in the future.

Procrastination Is Always There

Even the most productive people will procrastinate on something. For the rest of us, the question isn't if we procrastinate, it's how much and on which parts of the task. You may be a strong starter, a slow starter, get lost in the middle, or drop it at the end.

Procrastinating at the start means making excuses for why you can't begin right now. Procrastinating in the middle is losing steam, doing other things, intending to get back to it. Procrastinating at the end means not finishing the last steps because they're tedious or difficult. You want it perfect, and it never is.

I most often procrastinate in the middle. As soon as I run into problems I didn't expect, I abandon ship and look for new things to start. When you learn where your weakness lies, you can better prepare for it the next time.

Doom Deadlines and Doable Deadlines

Most people feel uneasy when they have an upcoming appointment or event they're nervous about. We're afraid of seeing the dentist or speaking in front of a crowd at a meeting, so we worry about how it will go.

When you have an upcoming appointment or event, you often enter waiting mode. You can't focus on anything because you're waiting. The appointment is in three hours. You should be productive, but you can't be.

Not all deadlines feel the same.

Doom deadlines are tasks you dread. Dentist appointments, phone calls to someone who makes you anxious, meetings with your boss, legal paperwork, and medical procedures. Anything that fills you with dread as it approaches.

Doable deadlines are events you're looking forward to. Lunch with a friend, picking your kid up from school, attending a concert you're excited about, or a video call with someone you haven't talked to in a while. These are positive events that you want to do, but they still create waiting paralysis.

Neurodivergent people take anticipation anxiety to another level. It can lead to complete paralysis.

Regulating our emotions isn't easy for us. When something is coming, our brains can't let it go. Our apprehension about the event leaves us stuck in waiting mode, doing nothing for the entire day, or, if we're very anxious about it, even the days leading up to it.

It doesn't always have to be negative anxiety. Sometimes we may welcome an event, like waiting for the airport shuttle to pick us up late in the afternoon, but we fritter away our day anticipating its arrival. We're so excited and fidgety that we can't focus enough to complete a single task all day.

Either way, whether it's doom or doable, the paralysis prevents us from getting anything done.

Treat the upcoming event itself as a deadline. Use the time leading up to it, rather than letting it paralyze you.

Let's say you need to leave for your dentist appointment in 60 minutes. That's your doom deadline. It's not artificial because you must leave your house within 60 minutes to make the appointment on time.

If you shift your thinking to say that 60 minutes is a hard deadline, you can complete one or more tasks in that time. You can't avoid the dentist appointment, but you can stop the hour before it from being a total loss and making your anxiety worse.

Neurodivergent people may struggle to estimate the time needed for tasks, so choose tasks where you're relatively sure how much time to allow. Try starting with the least desirable tasks that you can complete in 60 minutes.

You know from experience that taking out the trash, emptying the dishwasher, and sweeping the floors takes well under an hour.

Set an alarm to remind you when it's time to leave, in case you get sidetracked. If you expect a reminder or an alarm, you'll alleviate some of your anticipation anxiety about watching the clock and running late.

You'll go into your event less anxious because you haven't obsessed over it for the last hour.

If you're particularly prone to anticipation anxiety, try to schedule health appointments or work meetings, or any other events you're not keen on doing as early as possible in the day.

Every year, I have to get a full panel of bloodwork done. I don't have a choice. I know I have to do it. And I hate it.

As a needle-shy person, I would prefer to have every medical appointment at 6 a.m. to reduce the time I have to worry about it.

But usually, I end up with a time like 3:45 p.m., when I have to wait all day thinking about getting jabbed. I can't do anything else because I'm fixated on how much blood they'll have to take and how I hope I don't pass out...again.

So I sit and watch the clock until it's time to leave, and nothing gets done.

After the event, you may be so exhausted from your appointment that you feel like you can't do anything for the rest of the day. This post-event or conclusion anxiety can be from exhaustion, being overwhelmed because the event didn't go well, or being ecstatic because things went better than expected. Give yourself time to wind down and work through your emotions, but try to refocus on your remaining tasks.

Hard Start Principle

Sometimes the deadline is there, the consequence is real, and you know exactly what will happen if you don't do this. You still can't make yourself do it.

The **Hard Start Principle** works on one idea. You don't start the task. You start the smallest possible move toward it, and you let that move be enough to create the next one. This is for when everything else is working except the one task that won't.

You switched insurance last month and never canceled the old policy. Today is the last day before it auto-renews, and if that happens, and you finally do cancel, they'll hit you with another fee you can't afford. You've known this all week, and you're watching the clock run down.

You're on the couch, the phone is across the room, and you start building a case. You could do it later. Maybe the deadline isn't today. Maybe they'll give you a grace period. You don't have the account number handy anyway, and you'd have to dig out the paperwork. This would be easier tomorrow when you're more awake. For everyone else, this takes five minutes, but for you, it's an expedition, and the dread starts before you've even made the first move.

That's your brain negotiating its way out of something it doesn't want to do. It does this every time.

When you feel the negotiation starting, and you'll recognize it because it always starts the same way, ask yourself three things.

1. Does it have to be done?
2. What can your hands do right now toward this task?
3. Who am I doing this for?

Not should it be done or would it be nice to do? Does it have to be done, and does it have to be done now? If the answer is yes, your case for waiting doesn't hold up.

The phone is across the room and your hands can pick it up. Not make the call, just get the phone. Whatever your task is, think about the one physical thing your hands can do that moves you one step closer to it.

Sometimes doing it for yourself isn't enough, and that's okay. Think about everyone who depends on you getting this handled. Your kids. Your partner.

Your dog. The people and pets in your life who don't know the bill exists but will feel it if you get hit with a fee you can't afford.

That cancellation fee doesn't just cost you money. It comes out of something else, and you already know what that something else is. Every task you put off costs more time later, and that time has to come from somewhere. The future you will have one less thing hanging over your head.

That's the Hard Start Principle. You're not doing the whole task. You're making the first move.

Ready Window

Instead of forcing yourself to do things at scheduled times, wait for the moment when you're already thinking about it.

It happens without warning. Your friend asks if you want to shoot some hoops. Or you see a quick clip about origami and think, "I could do that." When that moment happens, that's when you do it. You're already interested, so go with it.

You want to exercise more. You've tried building the 6 a.m. gym habit, and it lasted all of four days. One Saturday afternoon, you think, "I kind of feel like going for a hike up the river." Go right then, while you're thinking about it. You won't go every day, but you'll go when the desire is there.

This approach works because you're not fighting against your natural rhythm. You're capturing the moments when motivation already exists instead of trying to manufacture it on a schedule that doesn't mesh with how you function.

For tasks without immediate consequences, do them when you're thinking about them. Don't wait for a better time or plan to do it later. That moment of natural motivation might not come back, so use it while it's there. When you're already thinking about it, starting is easier. But the tradeoff is inconsistency. You won't do the task every day or on a predictable schedule.

If you never think about something you want to do, maybe you don't actually want to do it. Or maybe the motivation will come eventually and you can wait for it instead of forcing something that isn't there.

This is partly about waiting to feel motivated, yes. But you're not waiting passively. You're noticing when motivation appears naturally and using it. Some people can build habits for things without immediate consequences. If you can't, this is your alternative.

It Won't Be Consistent

You won't work out every Monday, Wednesday, and Friday. You'll exercise on Tuesday and Thursday one week, Wednesday and Sunday the next, and five days the week after. Productivity advice hates inconsistency, but inconsistent exercise is better than no exercise, which is what happens when you try to force a schedule that doesn't work for you. Inconsistent effort still beats no effort.

***

Quick Take

- Use time bites. Small gaps between obligations are working time.
- Doom deadlines have real consequences. They force action when nothing else does.
- The Hard Start Principle: For a task that has to be done, ask three questions. Does it have to be done now? What can your hands do right now? Who am I doing this for?
- Catch the natural motivation in the Ready Window when it appears.

Ghost Habit #6

Create Your Workspace

Sleep Is Not Optional

Before you can do any real work, you need fuel.

While this doesn't happen as often anymore, I can't tell you how many times I'd get a new video game, hyperfocus on it, and play nonstop until I beat it. No sleep. No bathroom breaks. No food. Maybe a soda and chips, but nothing resembling real food. Not until I crushed the boss did I stop, even if that took nine hours and 175 restarts. Many of us know how that goes.

It's probably not unlike saying you'll just watch one more episode of an 18-season reality show and then you'll get up and make dinner, or you'll read one more chapter of a 450-page fantasy novel. Then suddenly you realize it's 1:30 a.m., you haven't eaten, you haven't done anything else, and you should have been in bed three hours ago.

You can say you run perfectly well on five hours of sleep a night, but that's true for very few people.

It may be what you've gotten used to, but it doesn't mean it's ideal.

Your body repairs itself when you sleep, and your brain needs a reset, though that's harder to come by when you're dealing with anxiety or working against a deadline. Lack of sleep can destroy your memory and concentration, making it harder to finish tasks. For people with ADHD, sleep disturbances affect around 60%. If that tracks with your experience, you're not imagining it.

If you have trouble sleeping, your bed should be for sleeping only. Don't watch Netflix, eat dinner, or bring your laptop to bed. You'll get to sleep sooner if you can associate your bed solely with sleep.

Waking up earlier gives you a jump on the day, but that only works if you go to bed earlier or already get too much sleep. If not, the lack of adequate rest will catch up with you.

We think we can skimp on our sleep during the week and catch up on the weekend. We look forward to those days with fewer demands. Unfortunately, when the weekend arrives, we may try to pack in so many fun activities that there aren't enough hours to fit them all in.

Instead, we stay up late, go out, or get engrossed in our hobbies because it's the weekend, and we want some fun. Inevitably, we wake up groggy on Monday morning and start the week already behind.

Hungry Brains Can't Focus

If a triple vanilla latte with caramel drizzle and an extra shot is your thing, then bottoms up. You can't concentrate if you're hungry, thirsty, or in need of a caffeine hit. But don't overdo it.

Caffeine in smaller doses may help. Like many things, this is a matter of trial and error. I found that consuming too much caffeine, especially late in the day, affects my sleep and, consequently, my productivity the next day. However, other neurodivergent individuals require caffeine throughout the day to sustain their energy levels. For yet another group, the tiniest sip will turn them into a shaky wreck, so they need to forgo it altogether.

You'll think more clearly when you're fully hydrated, so have a water bottle nearby.

Too much sugar and junk food affects your focus and concentration on top of everything else. As my expanding waistline proved, all those calories add up over time. It's not easy to change what you eat, but having better options nearby makes it easier to default to them.

At times, it might be a problem of not getting enough nutrition. Some of us have trouble remembering to eat during the day. If that's you, there are some strategies you can try. If you often forget to eat, write "Get a snack at 2 p.m." in the Everyday box on your **Task List**. Here are some other things that help:

- Stock healthy food in your kitchen.
- Have easy, no-prep foods, like granola bars, crackers, or fruit, near your desk for later in the day.
- Set reminders or alarms on your phone to alert you to eat.
- Prepare a week's worth of meals on one day, portion and freeze them, so you don't have to cook every day.
- Get a meal subscription service if you can afford it.
- Use an air fryer or a slow cooker to make food prep easier.

Everyone's eating needs are different. Find what makes it easier for you to eat regularly and stick with it.

You've Got to Move

If you work a desk job or sit in a vehicle, get up and move regularly. Even when working from home, where we have the freedom to move as we please, it's easy to stay on the couch for hours, especially if we get hyper-focused on our work.

If that's a problem, set reminders to get up regularly, eat meals, use the restroom, and stretch.

An activity as simple as walking outdoors can put you back into focus mode. It gets anxious energy moving, gives you fresh air, boosts your Vitamin D, and helps regulate your circadian rhythms.

You don't need any special equipment or an expensive gym membership, and you don't have to interact with anyone if you want to put in your earbuds and move. And if you're like me, put on a heavy-duty headset like airport runway workers wear so potential talkers get the hint that you're not up for a conversation.

Being sedentary for long periods can lead to serious health consequences. Even without hyperfocus pulling us into our activities, it's easy to sit for hours without moving. A Columbia University study suggests that merely walking for five minutes for every thirty minutes of sitting can counteract some of the negative health effects of prolonged sitting, lowering blood pressure, improving mood, and lowering blood sugar.

Small changes like that can make a significant impact on your overall activity level.

Take the stairs instead of the elevator. Park further away in the parking lot. Use a standing desk. Walk while you're talking on the phone. You're focused on the call, so you won't notice how much you're moving.

What Your Environment Is Doing to You

Much of your inability to focus can be traced to unsuitable working conditions. You may not be someone who can grab your laptop and work wherever you find an empty table.

We unconsciously absorb environmental cues that affect our mood and ability to focus. Blocking out the noise, lights, ringing phones, loud talkers, and the emotions you're feeling while working in uncomfortable conditions can make a huge difference in helping you get into a productive state of mind.

My ability to focus depends heavily on my work environment and surroundings. I can accomplish more with greater control. Blinding lights, loud music, constant interruptions, or the tense mood of a coworker can completely shut down my ability to work. Small environmental factors other people don't even notice can make the difference between a productive day and a wasted one.

Pregame Your Day

We want to pregame our day, but not in the wild college days sense of the word. Before you sit down to work, get four things in order. Clear whatever's grabbing at your attention, set up your workspace, get the sound right, and have everything you need within reach.

Get It Out of Your Head First

If you're thinking about something unrelated to the task you want to do, get it out of the way first. If it's a game you want to play, a fact you want to look up, or an earworm song you can't get out of your head, take care of that first. Play it, listen to it, or look it up. Otherwise, it'll interfere with your tasks because your mind won't let it go.

For the past decade, I've played an online strategy game full of quests that players must complete every 24 hours. Sometimes this game is the first thing I think about when I wake up. I play it on those days because I know my brain is too preoccupied to allow me to work on anything else.

Nothing in any online game requires my presence. I'm only accumulating points and prizes, but my brain has gotten hooked on that dopamine fix. Instead of fighting against it, I give in to it. But I only give it long enough for my brain to stop feeling compelled to do it.

Then I move on to my tasks when less weighs me down and pulls me away from the work I want to do.

There's always something to fight, build, or farm in gaming, so much so that some days I feel like I could play it non-stop for 24 hours. It's the same impulse in people who doomscroll social media. There's always something to keep you engaged and not doing the work you should be doing.

The Notifications Can Wait

Limit some of the noise coming at you through your phone. If your job or other commitments require you to use social media, cut down on the time you spend on it for personal use.

Stick to the platforms you need for work or school, and drop the rest. You don't have to be on all of them. Decide what apps are necessary and what are only wasting your time. Even if you don't use them, they're stealing a few seconds every time you scroll past them. Those seconds add up.

Turn off notifications that aren't time-sensitive when you're trying to focus. Use different ringtones to distinguish between emails or notifications that require an immediate reply and everything else you get.

I've turned off almost all of my notifications. The only ones I keep are banking and credit card alerts. Everything else can wait until I decide to check it.

Make It Your Space

Work in the place where you work best. On-site workers won't have as much freedom to select their workplace conditions, but if you're a student, a remote worker, or have a side gig, you have many options for how and where to work. Find a location that suits your projects and the conditions. A quiet home office, a converted garage, a corner of your bedroom, or your kitchen table can serve as a workspace if necessary. Others work better in public spaces, like a lively cafe, a busy coworking space, or a library.

Keep your desk, workbench, crafting table, or wherever you mix your sick beats free of unnecessary items. Clutter is a distraction, so get rid of it. Choose a comfortable chair, good lighting, and natural light if you have it.

A minimalist approach helps some people focus. Others do better surrounded by objects that calm or inspire them. The most important thing is to feel comfortable and free to work.

My primary workspace is a desk with two monitors. Having two monitors has changed how much I get done more than almost anything else

I've tried. I'm a visual thinker, so I work best when I can see my work and tasks spread across multiple screens. A single screen may work better for some people if it helps them zero in on a task, but if you've never tried two (or three), it's worth giving it a try.

Changing my desktop background daily helps me get into the work mindset. I set up a folder of rotating backgrounds and add new ones regularly. Whatever theme enables you to focus, sunny beaches, anime, cuddly kittens, cityscapes, change it to whatever puts you in the right frame of mind.

The Sounds of Productivity

One of the biggest motivators for you may be sound. Our ideal noise level is highly personal. Sound can enhance your concentration or completely distract you.

Do you usually work in a public or private space? For some, having someone in the room just quietly reading a book is distracting. It's harder to focus when a familiar person is there, even if all they can hear is a softly turning page or the barely audible growl of a hungry belly.

Household chores can be easier when you're entirely alone. Unless I'm in a room of total strangers at a café, being around people I know throws me off task. An empty house boosts my productivity when I'm in the mood to focus.

If you're distracted by all sound and work best in silence, try wearing earplugs or noise-canceling headphones, especially when working in busy offices or public places.

Silence can also be a focus killer. Hearing the clock tick and the taps on the keyboard can be maddening. If silence aggravates you, try drowning it out with something that doesn't pull your attention away from your work.

I work best with ambient noise in the background. Nature sounds, instrumental music, or the background noise of a busy street. I put on a coffeehouse sounds playlist when I'm working at home. Others might find the clattering cups, whirring coffee machines, and unintelligible chatter too lively. I find that constant background noise is perfect for writing or other creative projects. Try different options and see what works for the task you're doing.

Audiobooks, podcasts, or music with lyrics can distract people with auditory processing issues. Anything with intelligible words pulls your focus toward the story and away from your work.

White, pink, and brown noise are background sounds that many neurodivergent people find helpful for focus or sleep. White noise is the steady hiss most people know. Pink noise is softer and lower-pitched, closer to the sound of rain or rustling leaves. Brown noise is deeper, like rolling thunder. Many people with ADHD report that brown noise helps their concentration. Binaural beats are a newer option, rhythmic sounds designed to help focus and reduce stress and anxiety. Try them all out and see which ones your brain responds to.

What helps with one task may not help with another. Experiment with different types of sound, or none at all.

Make the Boring Ones Bearable

While noise levels can undermine our ability to focus on an intense task, the opposite is true for unexciting tasks like washing dishes or sweeping the floor. Tasks that don't require intense concentration or creativity.

Why do you rarely see a jogger without earbuds? Running 10 miles every day gets old fast, especially when you run the same route day after day. If you can entertain yourself, you'll make it more bearable.

Find an audiobook, podcast, or playlist that holds your attention, put on your headphones, and start on something you've been avoiding. It might change everything about that task.

It's Not the Space for You

Maybe you've got roommates who don't have an inside voice. Your kids interrupt you every 10 minutes. You're in an open office where everyone's constantly talking and gossiping, and your coworkers walking up to your desk is perfectly fine whenever they feel like it.

You can't make the roommates quiet, the kids disappear, or the coworkers respect your boundaries.

Those noise-canceling headphones I mentioned earlier aren't just for focus. Now use them for survival. Even cheap ones help. Play instrumental music, white noise, or brown noise, anything that gives you something consistent to focus on instead of random interruptions.

Visible signals help, too. Headphones on means don't interrupt. Even if you're not playing any sound at all, potential chatters don't know that. The door closed means come back later. Specific hours written on your door or desk mean I'm available then, not now. Not everyone will respect these signals, but many will, and that gives you some relief.

If everyone's loud from 9 a.m. to 5 p.m., work at 6 a.m. or 10 p.m. I know it's not fair. But if it's the only way to get quiet time, then that's what you have to do.

If your current space is unusable, go somewhere else entirely. Go to the library, the coffee shop, or sit in your car. Anywhere that's not your house or office. Sometimes escape is the only option.

You're not going to get as much done in a chaotic environment as you would be in one more suitable to your preferences. That's the reality. So don't expect to get the same amount done. Do one thing instead of three. One hour of focus is better than none.

Do what you can with the situation you have.

Do It Now, Thank Yourself Later

You're feeling good, and you have a free Saturday afternoon with no pressing demands. Should you play the video game you love or read a few chapters in your textbook due the following week? The obvious answer is the game, right? But if you're in the headspace to read, doing it now means you won't have to force it later when the deadline is closing in, and you might not be able to concentrate. You get the work done while it's easier for you. You play the game without guilt afterward. That's paying it forward to yourself.

Apps and games are not always the time-wasters they're made out to be. An hour of Candy Crush can calm you down when you're overwhelmed. Streaming a movie provides you with the mindless entertainment break you need. But running to them when you're avoiding something with a real deadline and real consequences is a different matter. If you need the escape, take it. If you're in a mindset where focus is possible, that's the time to make the most of it.

***

Quick Take

- You need fuel. Sleep, food, and movement.
- Your environment affects your output. Set it up to work for you.
- Notifications are interruptions. Turn them off when you need to focus.
- If your workspace isn't right for you, find one that is.

Ghost Habit #7

Stay in the Zone (Then Get Out)

Before You Go All In

When making monumental decisions, recognize that, as neurodivergent individuals, we're sometimes impulsive and can jump the gun, like overspending or quitting a job abruptly. You may need to put the brakes on if you're prone to diving in headfirst.

I lean toward impulsivity and tend to jump in with both feet, hands, body, and all. When I make a decision, I think it's the greatest decision I've ever made, and it must be done today. Usually, a week or two later, it's come to a screeching halt, and I'm either stuck with it or frantically searching for ways to get out of it.

I once decided on a whim to apply to graduate school. A few days before the application period ended, I came across information online about a program I was interested in, and I went all in. I submitted my documents within the week and was accepted a few weeks later.

Of course, I thought that decision would propel my life in a new direction. I wish I had thought more about the timing or discussed it with others, but I was too impulsive.

I should have waited until my life was more settled. It cost me time and money I couldn't afford, and while it wasn't disastrous, I learned a hard lesson.

It's All or Nothing

Whether we like it or not, a lot of us are all-or-nothing personalities. You might be a fence sitter who's scared to make a decision. Things that should get the go-ahead after determining they're in our best interest often don't because we're paralyzed by fear. So they sit, and we wait, putting our lives on hold. You can be a jumper who leaps before they look. Things that check our boxes can get the green light before they should, because they feel right in the moment. Some of us are one or the other, depending on the situation.

When we feel motivated, we often want to do it all today. Whatever unusual hobby, DIY project, or travel plan comes to mind. No matter how long it takes us to plan it the right way, we'd rather skip the planning and go for broke. We don't have a slow mode when it comes to our new obsessions. That would take too much time. We want to learn to knit, code in C++, or water ski, and become experts as soon as possible.

Maybe that's because we know that's all our attention spans allow. Or we've fallen in love with the idea of being a knitter, a software developer, or a water skier far too soon. We don't yet fully know what it involves, but we can already see ourselves with that identity. We like it.

The real work begins, and we don't stick with it. It's not happening fast enough before the boredom sets in.

Hold back on investing too many resources in your new idea until you've committed to it. Don't decide you want to be a scuba diver, then go all in and buy thousands of dollars' worth of equipment, only to later admit to yourself you're terrified of deep water.

Do you have the time, the budget, the sustained interest, or are you falling in love with the idea of it? Sleep on it. Talk your decision over with someone who might see what you can't. Try to give it 48 hours before you commit.

The Research Spiral

There's a side of all-or-nothing that looks like doing everything right. You found something you're excited about. Maybe it's not scuba gear. It's historical weaponry. You're being responsible by learning all about it first.

You watch every YouTube video on the subject. You join the subreddits. You read the beginner guides, then the intermediate ones, and then the Discord threads where people argue about the right way to do it. You have 214 tabs open (which I've actually had open) and a notes app full of things you want to try. You're ready to start.

Except you never do, because the learning is where the dopamine is. Every new piece of information feels like you're making headway. It has the appearance of work without the risk of putting something out into the world and finding out you're not as good at it as you thought. The research phase is safe.

The problem now is that you've already told everyone you're into historical weaponry. You were excited, and you talked about it, which felt almost as good as doing it. Now you've quietly dropped it, but you didn't inform them. Your mom still asks you how the podcast you were going to do is coming along. Your friend keeps sending you articles about medieval swords. You smile and say you've been busy, which is true, and you don't mention that you've stopped reading about it.

At some point, the interest drops off completely, usually right around when you'd actually have to do something hard, and all of it goes cold. The tabs stay open for a while. Then you close them. A few months later, you remember what you were going to do.

If you recognize this pattern, one way through it is to set a hard limit on how long you're allowed to prepare before you have to produce something, anything, even if it's terrible. A week of research, then you create one thing. You write the first paragraph. You record the first video. You cook the dish. It doesn't matter how bad it is. You need to get something out before your interest evaporates.

You know the point when it stopped feeling new.

If the interest couldn't survive long enough to make one thing, the fantasy of it was always more appealing than the reality.

Your Three Levels of Focus

Getting important things done requires a steady level of focus. Most of us have more than one level of attention when we can focus at all. For me, there are three. Focus, **superfocus**, and hyperfocus.

At times, I can focus. That's minimal focus, where I have to use extra energy to stay on task, but I can get through my tasks without much distraction. Most household chores and lighter work tasks are in this category. I'm motivated to finish them and can sustain my focus long enough to get through them.

It's easier to concentrate if I'm more interested in the task. This is similar to what experts call a flow state. That's a more intense focus, or what I describe as my superfocus. I don't have to try to think about the task because I'm fully absorbed in the activity. I can pull myself out of it relatively quickly if I need to switch gears.

Beyond that is the highest level of focus, or hyperfocus, where the task at hand is the only thing I can think about. The task or project almost becomes a compulsion. These are times when I can easily pull an all-nighter. It's the opposite problem I have with my everyday executive function. I'm so consumed that I have to force myself to take breaks to attend to basic human needs like eating and sleeping.

While hyperfocus doesn't happen often for me, I can get through several days of work in a few hours when it does. Unfortunately, keeping a balance takes tremendous mental effort. Hyperfocus takes a toll on my overall well-being.

Focus = Minimal attention + moderate motivation
Superfocus = High attention + engaged motivation
Hyperfocus = Extreme attention
+ obsessive motivation

When I need to do serious work, I aim for superfocus. I may not be able to control it, but that's the goal. That's my ideal level of focus, where I'm in the zone. I can do my tasks efficiently without reminders. I'm fully interested and eager to get them done. Anti-tasks don't faze me, and I do more in less time. It's similar to hyperfocus in that I don't feel the passage of time, but I can quickly leave the task if something important arises.

Getting Into Superfocus

You can't force superfocus or manufacture it. But you can set up conditions that increase the likelihood.

Work on things you're interested in. You won't get into superfocus on something that bores you, and forcing it won't make it happen. If the task is unavoidable, find an angle on it that engages you enough to start.

Superfocus breaks easily. One interruption, one missing tool, one "where did I save that file?" moment, and you're out of it. Before you start, make sure all your tools are within reach. Pull up the information you need. Put your phone on silent. Have your materials ready to go.

Start when you're already thinking about the task. If you're putting away the groceries and you suddenly feel like you can make that dreaded phone call you've been avoiding, do it then. Not whenever your calendar says you should. If you can, work when the interest is there, not when the schedule says so.

Don't fight it when your superfocus wears off. When it ends, it ends. Suddenly, the task gets harder. You're looking at the clock and getting distracted.

That's the signal that you're done. Take a break and come back later. Forcing it past its natural end makes everything harder and burns you out faster.

On, Off, and Everything in Between

Let's say you want to paint your living room a stunning new color for spring. At first, you think about how fabulous your space will look with a trendy new color splashed on its walls. Before you know it, you find yourself at the paint store, gleefully perusing the names of the color swatches, deciding whether you feel more in tune with a Sand Flea Sarcoline or a Citrus Gamboge. This is so much fun, you say to yourself. Look at how many choices there are.

With the intensity of a veteran FBI forensic investigator, you pore over the colors and deduce a winner. Without hesitation, you're on your way home with a trunk full of paint and supplies, eager to start.

Now you're like a cheetah throwing back the energy drinks as you rearrange the furniture and take down the family photos of your great-greats and your framed 2nd-grade artwork. You cover the floors, tape up the outlets and molding, sweep, dust, set out your supplies, and then, a few hours into your project, it hits you. Who knew there was this much work to paint a room? You feel like you're losing interest.

But now, it's time to prepare the walls. You haven't even put a drop of color on the walls yet. You suit up and start to sand the walls. You're feeling more distracted.

As you glance out the window, your mind drifts to all the fun things you could be doing out there instead of sweating in an air mask in a cavernous, dusty room. You look around and realize just how much wall space you have.

The next day, you wake up, and your motivation is barely there. The excitement was in the idea and vision you had in your head of the finished room, not so much in scraping off decades of old paint.

It's not going to be as easy as you thought. And since your walls aren't perfectly straight and you're not a professional painter, it won't look like the Scandinavian showroom you originally envisioned.

Now, your only choices are to abandon the project and leave it half done, power through and hope it looks acceptable, or pay someone to finish the job. None of these options is good for you.

When to Bounce

Sometimes you can't stay on task no matter what you do. You sit down to write that report, and five minutes later, you're checking emails. Then you remember you need to schedule an appointment. Then you notice your floor needs sweeping, so you get the broom. Then you're back to the report for three minutes before something else catches your attention.

When you can't stay on one task, you can fight it and accomplish nothing, or go with it and get something done.

If you're bouncing between tasks and making progress on several of them, even if you don't finish any, you're getting things done. Fifteen minutes on the report, five minutes on emails, three minutes organizing, ten minutes on laundry. By the end of the day, you've nudged four tasks along instead of none.

Productive bouncing means each time you switch, you're working on something that needs to be done. Reports, emails, and sweeping are all tasks you'll eventually need to do.

Procrastination bouncing means you're sweeping the floor when it doesn't need it to avoid the hard task. You're checking social media to avoid the email. You're moving around but accomplishing nothing important.

When you're switching between tasks and getting things done, keep going.

If you're staying busy but nothing meaningful is getting done, you're procrastinating. Stop what you're doing and try to focus on the hard task for five minutes. Then, if you still can't stay on it, let it bounce again.

When an anti-task appears while you're trying to work, you know what to do. Figure out what need it's meeting, give it a defined amount of time, and get back. Some days, the anti-task wins and the work doesn't get done. That's a hard day, and your **Task List** will still be there tomorrow.

Your Output Matters

You can do 10-hour days of research, outlines, drafts, editing, brainstorming, reading, watching YouTube, completing courses, tinkering with your website, organizing your studio, ordering supplies, and planning your calendar on a project you're already deep into. And while everything you're doing is slowly moving you closer to your goal, if it's busy work, unnecessary work you're doing to "feel" productive, or if you're delaying the hard stuff, or you're afraid to complete it and send it out to the world, then it's not progress.

Some projects have high learning curves. On any subject, we can spend 1,000 hours reading, watching YouTube videos, and searching websites for the answers we need. We fool ourselves into thinking this is the same as being productive. Most of the tasks we want to do are not very complicated. They are more tedious than complex. We indulge only in the parts of the project that are enjoyable to us, instead of pushing through the task.

Other tasks we might want to do that take real time and dedication. A remodeling project. Restoring an old car. Starting a community group. Finishing a series of artworks. For any of these, there are always parts of the project that don't suit our interests or abilities as much as others, and while you want to complete it, not everything will be fun and engaging.

If you're who this book is for, finishing one thing is already a win.

When Something Derails Your Day

When we get sidetracked by something unavoidable, we often don't know what to do next. I expect my day to be ABCD. But then trouble, T, enters the picture. Now my day is ABCT. D is gone, thrown off by something I didn't plan for.

Once we've dealt with the unexpected change, we have to regain our focus and set aside any negative emotions it's brought. While dealing with the trouble, keep the previous task in the back of your mind as much as possible. Limit new interruptions. Zero in on the most engaging part of the task to ease yourself back into it. If you can't get back to that task at all, work on something related or go to your Task List.

When you take a break, stay with an interesting part of the project while you're away. A problem you're working out, something you want to research, anything that keeps you in it while you're doing something else. Stay in it as much as possible so that coming back is easier.

Work until you've finished or until you've lost interest, whichever comes first. When staying on task gets difficult, find the part of the project that's most interesting right now and focus there. Read over what you've already done. Remember why you wanted to do this in the first place. Switch to a different part of it. You might find it easier to come back to something when it feels new again, so sometimes stepping away for a while is the right call.

If you can't get back to it for an extended time, leave yourself notes before you go. What you were thinking, what comes next, what sources you were using, what measurements you took, what page you were on. Write it down while you're still in it because you won't remember it when you return. Give yourself instructions for what to do first when you come back.

Stop at a place where you can pick it up easily. Just as you don't want to replay an entire level of your fighting game because you had to dip out on one mission, you don't want to waste time reviewing everything before you can move forward. Stop at a natural breaking point and you'll spend less time getting back up to speed.

Your Needs Come First

When people tell me to just do it, whatever "it" is, I have to choose what's most important because I'll face the consequences later. I can't focus on something I'm not interested in for 8 or 10 hours a day. That's a guaranteed breakdown.

Sustained attention comes at a high price. My ADHD doesn't care that the clock says I have to finish a task. It's as much a part of me as my farsightedness or my wonky knee from playing high school basketball. I work with it.

I know what the real costs of sustained focus are because I paid them almost daily. I experienced a sort of breakdown at my first "grown-up" job out of college, where I worked rotating shifts on a loud, dusty factory floor, often with only one day off a week. The stress was overwhelming, and words can't express how much I despised that job. I managed to last a couple of years, but I was an emotional wreck.

If I wasn't working, I was sleeping or unsuccessfully managing my anxiety. I was barely eating. My weeks were so long that I hardly had time for anything else. It felt like living in a persistent fog. But society told me I had a good, well-paying job, and I should shut up and be grateful to have it.

If I'd been realistic about my abilities, I'd never have taken a job in that field. I could have saved a lot of emotional distress. In hindsight, even today, I feel like I completely lost those years of my life.

When people say money can't buy happiness, maybe that's true. But money shouldn't buy your unhappiness either.

I know that's easy to say and nearly impossible to do. When you've got rent, healthcare bills, debt, and dependents, leaving a toxic job isn't realistic. There are times when survival means staying in situations that hurt us.

If you have any option at all, prioritize your health over the paycheck. No job is worth destroying yourself. Sometimes you stay because you have to survive.

The Signs You're Done Even If You Think You're Not

"Keep at it for as long as possible" doesn't mean "work until you collapse." There's a difference between stopping because you're distracted and stopping because you need to stop.

Stop when the quality is dropping. You've been at this for hours, and now you're making mistakes and having to redo things. You're past the point of usefulness. Stop.

Stop when you're forcing it. You're no longer in superfocus. You're barely in focus. You're grinding through on willpower alone. That willpower is going to run out, probably in the next 10 minutes. Stop before it does.

Stop when you've forgotten to eat or sleep. If you look up and it's been six hours since you last ate, stop. If you've been awake all day, and at this since 10 p.m., and it's now 4 a.m., stop. Your body needs food and sleep more than your project needs another hour of focus.

Stop when you're in hyperfocus and can't tell anymore. This is the hardest one to catch because hyperfocus is deceptive. While you're in it, you feel good, like you can keep going because you're on a roll. But you're not. Set an alarm. When it goes off, stop and check in. Have you eaten? Have you moved? Have you blinked? If the answer is no, stop.

Nothing is so important that you should sacrifice your health for it. Not work, not a deadline, not a project you're excited about.

***

Quick Take

- Ride superfocus as long as it lasts. When quality drops or you're forcing it, stop.
- Superfocus: fully engaged, can step away when needed.

- Hyperfocus: can't stop, lose track of time and body needs.
- When you can't stay on one task, productive bouncing beats paralysis.
- Busy work isn't output. Make sure you're making progress.
- When something derails your day, limit new interruptions and ease back in.
- Nothing is worth your health. Know when to quit.

Ghost Habit #8

Take the Downtime You Need

You Need More Rest Than You Think

We need a lot of downtime. You can be highly productive when you're on, but you need significant recovery time to get back to that level. We're consistently inconsistent by nature. Our lives swing between distraction, focus, burnout, and recovery.

Sometimes that cycle stretches across weeks or months. Things go well for a while. Tasks get done, and you feel like you've finally figured something out. Then one day it stops. Without warning, with no obvious cause, you're back to doing nothing. The cycle always ends the same way. You rest, and you come back.

This is one reason many of us can't sustain full-time traditional employment long-term without paying a high price. We may do it well for a while, but we can't maintain that pace unless we have support, and it suits how we function. Temporary jobs, part-time work, or freelancing may be the more realistic path. Not everyone is cut out for a five- or six-day workweek.

What Real Rest Looks Like

This is different from the sleep, food, and movement basics in Ghost Habit #6. Those keep you fueled for daily work. Recovery is what happens after you've been depleted, after a crash, a burnout, or a hyperfocus binge that ran you into the ground.

Scrolling social media for three hours leaves you more drained than when you started. Here's what real rest looks like:

Doing nothing. Sitting or lying on the couch without sleeping. It feels wrong because we're told that's lazy and we should always be doing something, but sometimes you need to completely power down.

Physical movement that doesn't feel like exercise. Walking, dancing, swimming, rollerblading, anything that gets you moving without feeling like you're doing a workout.

Creative activities like drawing, playing music, building something, writing for fun. You're not doing these for money or for anyone else.

Time outside with no other purpose than to enjoy nature. Sit in the yard, walk in the park, watch the birds, or look at the clouds. Get away from devices and noise for an afternoon.

Actual sleep in a dark room without screens for as long as your body needs it.

True rest should leave you feeling at least slightly better than when you started.

The Hyperfocus Crash

If you've been in hyperfocus mode, regular recovery isn't enough. The crash that follows hyperfocus is different.

Everything stops. You won't be able to start tasks or focus on anything. You'll feel like you've used up every bit of energy you had, and now there's nothing left.

This happens to everyone who hyperfocuses. When you hyperfocus, you're running at maximum capacity for extended periods, burning through dopamine, attention, and willpower at an unsustainable rate. Eventually, you run out.

You can't prevent it. Planning for it is the next best thing.

Don't schedule important tasks right after finishing a big project. You won't be functional for the rest of the day, possibly longer.

Give yourself permission to do nothing. Watch TV, listen to music, eat simple food, and sleep a lot. You accomplished something significant. Let yourself recover without beating yourself up.

Give it time, and the crash will end. Usually within a few days, though sometimes longer if you really pushed hard.

There's another kind of crash entirely where no single project is to blame. Just weeks or months of getting through your days, handling obligations, fighting the chaos, and keeping your life from falling apart. That steady daily effort burns through fuel too. Do it long enough and you crash anyway.

If you've hit a wall and can't point to why, you have nothing left. Rest without guilt and come back when you're ready. The missing reason makes the guilt worse, but you don't need one to deserve rest.

Pacing Your New Interests

Pacing yourself when a new interest takes over is one of the hardest things to do because you can't stop thinking about it. You're primed to go all in, but you can learn to step back and temper that impulse.

Ask yourself whether the time you're spending on it is bringing anything positive to your life, and whether you're neglecting the people and pets who need you.

Ask friends to say something when they notice signs of **hyperfixation**, like when you've disappeared into a new interest for days. Remove the cues from your environment that pull you into it. Make the new interest harder to access until you've done what needs doing first.

If you can slow it down, the interest lasts longer, and you can delay the crash.

You Need People in Your Corner

Most of us have spent years trying to figure this out on our own. Having even one person who gets it makes a difference. Not necessarily a therapist, though that helps too. Someone who knows what you're dealing with and isn't going to tell you to apply yourself and try harder.

Start with your circle. Friends, family, coworkers, roommates. Anyone who already knows your situation and isn't dismissive of it. Expand from there when you're ready. Volunteer groups, community support groups, and online communities. The neurodivergent communities on Reddit, Discord, and Facebook groups are large, and people there understand what you're describing without needing an explanation. If you'd rather meet people in person, Meetup can help you find local groups.

Figure out what you need before you start looking. One person to bounce ideas off is different from a group dealing with similar problems, which is different from someone who'll check in on you. You don't need a network. You need something that fits what you're missing.

Support goes both ways. Give your time when you can and set boundaries so it doesn't drain you. Some people will take much more than they give and call it friendship. Pay attention to how you feel after spending time with someone. If you're questioning their motives, trust your gut.

Nobody Does It Alone

As much as people who have "made it" like to say they pulled themselves up by their bootstraps, that's not true. There's hardly anything we do that we haven't received help with at some point.

Parents pay living expenses or tuition. Scholarships allow some of us to attend better schools or school at all. A friend helps you get a job at their employer or lets you crash on their couch between jobs. A teacher writes the recommendation that gets you into grad school. Someone lends you their car when yours isn't running, or lets you use their garage to start your business.

Nobody who claims they made it entirely on their own is telling the full story.

We are born as tiny, entirely dependent humans. None of us could have survived childhood without the care and help of others. That doesn't stop when we grow up. Every single one of us has benefited from others.

Sometimes it takes one minor setback and no one to help you to turn your world upside down.

Not long out of college, I had a coworker who had no choice but to leave work early because her child was sick. After making frantic phone calls, she couldn't find anyone to pick up the child from school, so she left and was subsequently fired. One common event can drastically change your life when you have no one to help you.

Saying No Isn't Selfish

Many of us are people pleasers. We go out of our way to be helpful to others or take on tasks that cause us internal turmoil because we're empathetic, sometimes to a fault, and want to make others happy. We have to deal with the fallout from taking on too many assignments or unsuitable tasks, often at the expense of our downtime. When we do this, our stress and anxiety levels affect other areas of our lives, pushing us toward burnout, depression, or physical distress.

It's good, even unselfish, to say no to projects you know aren't right for you. You're doing them a favor if you can pass it along to someone who can give it the proper attention it deserves. Don't feel guilty about that.

You may feel the need to go above and beyond due to your perfectionism. Trust your gut feeling and say no. You can't do everything for everyone. Take care of yourself first.

You Don't Get Those Hours Back

You may feel pushed into taking any job, even if it's all wrong for you, because you need the money. You may struggle to find a career and muddle through, earning a living but never finding your niche. The rest of your time is mostly yours, but you don't know what to do with that either.

I was in this predicament. I had hours to devote to tasks, but I had no direction. I knew vaguely what I wanted to do and where I wanted to be, but I wasn't sure how to get there, and I couldn't make the opening move. My inability to begin cost me valuable time, which was a lost fortune if I viewed it as money.

We don't randomly toss our money on the ground or into the trash. We try to be careful with how we spend it. We've learned its importance because it's a limited resource that's hard to acquire. We try to spend it only on what we need or want.

Time is the same, but we're more carefree with it. Those 24 hours belong to you, but they're depleted daily. You don't get do-overs, and you can't stash them away for the future.

We don't think about time until something interrupts our assumption that it'll always be there. A health scare. A diagnosis. A friend who suddenly can't do the things they used to. Those moments are gut punches you don't forget.

That's not to scare you into getting a regular, mundane 9-to-5 office job. It's to jolt you out of your comfortable life, especially if your life now isn't what you want.

Every hour you spend mindlessly scrolling TikTok is an hour you didn't spend on things you'd be proud of doing. Not a single person at 90 years old will look back and say, "I'm most proud of spending 42,877 hours on TikTok." That's not unreasonable, given that the average user spends over 2 hours a day on the app.

Something Always Gets Neglected

Everything competes for your time. Work, health, relationships, rest. When one of them takes over, the others start breaking down, and usually you don't notice until you're already burned out, isolated, or running on empty.

It's never perfectly equal, but we try. Some interests may take more or less of your attention at different stages of your life, but nothing should shut out everything else.

Nowadays, it's easy to feel like we should spend more time on our work life. But that's a futile effort. We can always take on one more task at work or spend one more hour building our careers to make more money. We can become stressed-out workaholics with no outside life, and even then, it won't be enough because it never ends. There's always more to do.

Balance looks different for everyone, and it shifts over time. What works for you now may look completely different in a few years.

Progress on Your Own Timeline

How often have you heard someone say, "If you want to do it, then just do it." As if doing the task you're struggling to do is as simple as snapping your fingers.

I can't put myself in that headspace. If I'm forced to do a task when I'm not ready, I'll either spend double or triple the time it should take or do an awful job, which leaves me ashamed of my work.

If I have to write a detailed email reply when I'm not in the mood, I'll stare blankly at the screen and eventually write a few words. I'll reread them repeatedly, playing out how the receiver will interpret them. The minutes tick by, and I've gotten nowhere. It's hardly an efficient use of time.

Forcing yourself to do a task you're not into rarely leads to stellar results. You don't feel better when you push yourself to do something you don't want to do.

Sure, you can say you put in eight hours by setting a timer and sitting at your desk. But how many productive hours did you get if you daydreamed about what you'll be doing on the weekend, or you read the same chapter over and over because you couldn't focus?

Time spent trying isn't everything. If you're making progress and still motivated, then you're succeeding. How far you've come is a better measure than how much you've checked off.

***

Quick Take

- You will crash. It's part of how you function.
- Rest without guilt. Recovery is not optional.
- Real rest is not scrolling. It's doing nothing, moving, creating, and being outside.
- After hyperfocus, give yourself time to recover before starting anything hard.
- Having even one person who gets it makes a difference.
- Measure yourself by how far you've come, not your checklist.

You're Doing Your Best

A Different Starting Line

The voice in your head tells you you're still not doing enough. Going at your own pace sounds reasonable until you look around and see everyone else doing more and doing it better. Or at least that's how it looks.

The system, school, work, social media, the whole productivity culture machine, was built around neurotypical people. That's the norm. And if your brain doesn't work that way, you're already behind before you even think about making your first move.

Your road has more obstacles and fewer people who know how to help you navigate them. You may have spent years trying to figure out why things that seemed easy for everyone else were so hard for you. Years of being told to make more of an effort, focus better, and just do it. By the time you're an adult, the doubt is a part of you.

But it didn't materialize out of nowhere. You watched other people do effortlessly what takes everything you have. You failed at something the world told you was easy. Social media showed you what success looked like, and it didn't look anything like your life.

We're not comparing ourselves to people with the same circumstances. We're comparing ourselves to people with better equipment who got a head start and never had to fight their own brains just to reach the starting line.

We're told we have to be out there creating content and selling ourselves. We broadcast to the world that we're experts in whatever field we want to succeed in. We "fake it 'til we make it." Behind that facade are burnout, stress, anxiety, and the constant worry that if you don't play the game well enough, you're falling behind.

You think you're not beautiful, rich, or smart enough. If you're not spending all day on Instagram, no one will like you, and you'll end up living in a one-room apartment with your 14 cats. You start to believe your self-worth is determined by followers and likes.

Stop at 90%

Many of us with neurodivergent conditions are told we're perfectionists. We can't let things go. We set excessively high standards, and we refuse to accept anything less than flawless execution. People will roll their eyes and tell you to do it, but that doesn't work. We obsess over the most minor details. It's like telling someone to lift 500 lb. weights above their head. It's not going to happen.

You've done the bulk of your project, but now you have to finish it and put it out into the world. We should aim for 90% completion. This doesn't mean precisely 90%, but rather when you realize you're spending time on the task without making any measurable progress.

If your work requires precision because mistakes have real consequences, 90% is not your target. You already know that. This is for everything else. The email you've rewritten six times and the project that's been sitting there for months don't need to be perfect. For those, 90% done and out in the world is better than perfect and still sitting on your desk.

In my high school, a 90% was a low A. You don't need Outstanding when Excellent is enough. It might not be your absolute best work ever, but it's top-notch compared to getting a C or D or receiving a zero by not doing it at all. It's OK to be less than perfect if it means we get something done.

Accept that it's essentially done once you complete 90% of the task. The first thing you can do is take a short break from it. If you come back to it and make significant advances, continue. But if you're rehashing the old, call it quits.

You know you're at 90% if you've covered all the main points or benchmarks you intended, and you're repeating the same work over and over, or you don't feel like you're making forward progress. If someone else can tie up the loose ends, great. If it's all on you, you either power through it or turn it in as is.

Make it presentable and consider it done. You check for any glaring mistakes or major problems and move on. This is especially true for written projects. Proofread it and hit Send. For a lot of us, that's the harder part.

More time doesn't make it better. You'll procrastinate anyway and throw together something subpar before the deadline. At some point, more time means more second-guessing.

We want to keep working on it indefinitely and find it hard to accept that there's realistically no more to do. We can grind away forever on what we think is the last 10%. Minor improvements can make a slight difference in overall quality, but they won't offset the time and energy you spend continuously editing and improving your work.

It's never going to be exactly what you envisioned when you began the project. Our fear of judgment gets in the way, telling us it's still not ready for the world.

The Project That Won't Go Away

As perfectionists know, finishing a task means we can't change it if something new comes up, if you get a great new idea to improve it, or you realize you made a mistake and need to rework it. You can only make a first impression once. That's all part of our task paralysis.

When you first decided this was the project you would do, you couldn't imagine all the different elements that would affect the outcome. Because, well, you hadn't done the project yet. But you're probably like most people who feel disappointed when the finished product doesn't match what you imagined. So you continue to revise and give it more time until you feel it's ready for the world.

Your perfectionism keeps pushing the finish line further and further away.

Indecision and the "What Ifs"

Indecisiveness and judgment are aspects of perfectionism that affect your ability to get things done. Much of our indecision stems from "what if" thinking. You can't choose a path because "What if something in my current circumstances changes?

"What if I lose my scholarship?"

"What if I get a bad performance review?"

When you're wired this way, remote possibilities carry the same weight as likely ones, which is why decisions are so hard to make.

"What if I break my leg while jogging and can't walk for two months?"

"What if my car breaks down, I can't get it fixed, I have no transportation, and I can't get to my job?"

They cause you to keep looking at alternatives in case you get a different outcome.

"What if the app I build gets so popular that Big Tech wants to snap it up? Maybe I should take more time to think about my marketing plans and get it just right before I begin to code it?"

What if you choose the wrong major? What if you accept the wrong job? What if you're not ready to expand your business? What if you're moving to the wrong city? What if you're going in the entirely wrong direction in your life?

You're afraid it's not right for you, so you do nothing, which wastes valuable time. When your perfectionism and overthinking paralyze you, you won't act because you can't be 100% certain. You don't have a Magic 8-ball to see how it'll all work out, so you do nothing.

Work Gets Judged but Do It Anyway

There's no way around it because work will be judged. You may delay launching the podcast you've wanted to start for years because you're afraid of the reviews you'll get. Once it's gone live, people will hear it and judge you based on the work you produce. We all know what it's like when our work is displayed for everyone to see. It's not easy, and sometimes it's terribly painful to hear criticism, even when it's constructive.

We're judged by society every day, from our behavior to our appearance to other factors entirely beyond our control.

Consider the source. The person criticizing you may only see a small part of what you've done, may be missing context, or may be working from their own opinions, which are not facts.

You also judge people. You know you do. We can make hasty critical judgments, and some of us are guilty of being very direct in our language. We don't always consider how the other person will take it, so it's important to remember this when we're on the receiving end.

No matter what you do, you'll always get those who criticize everything they see. It's impossible to avoid those who leave a "You're dumb" comment on everything they read. If Albert Einstein were around in the social media age, he'd get them, too.

As harsh as it is, we have to get used to them if we want to keep going. At some point, you have to put it out there anyway.

The Negative Thoughts That Won't Quit

I've learned it takes me longer than others to finish projects, so I build in extra time. I don't put myself on the same timeline as other people. When I read about someone who developed an app, wrote an entire fantasy book series, or conquered three languages in six months, I recognize that I can't compare myself to their success.

Often, we look back and see that someone younger than us or newer to the field accomplished something that may have taken us several years, or even an entire decade, to do. We feel inadequate. It's that same sinking feeling you get when you look through your college alum newsletter and see your former classmates nominated for major awards or at the top of their professions.

We don't know the circumstances of how the successful person "made it." It could be a lot of hard work and perseverance. However, it may also be that nepotism, family connections, wealth, and access to superior education or training played a hand in it. Or maybe it's unbelievable timing and good fortune. It may be nearly impossible for us to reach the same level because we don't have the same circumstances, no matter how much hard work we put into it.

I recall several times in my life things weren't going well, and I later wondered why I didn't fix them when I had the chance. I could have changed many things if I had known then what I know now. I feel guilty, or at least regretful, over those things. But when I snapped out of my pity party, I realized I wasn't ready to change it at the time. Even if someone I sincerely trusted had offered me help, I probably would have shrugged and said, "Sure, thanks," and continued doing what I was doing.

When you start with a negative image of yourself, it's hard to look at another person's accomplishments and use them as a source of positive motivation to do more in your own life. You'll only compare yourself negatively.

"I'll never be able to do that."

"They're so much smarter than I am."

"They've got their life together, and mine is a dumpster fire."

You're not going to see the hardships they went through. If you've become skilled at hiding your struggles from the world, perhaps they have, too. If you put yourself out there, especially on social media, wouldn't you try to hide your flaws and show only your most interesting side and greatest accomplishments? If you'd do that, don't you think they all do it? In that way, they're really no different than you.

We are all flawed. We see all the negatives in our actions and talk ourselves out of what we're working on. Comparing yourself to other people is self-sabotage. When you do this and already struggle with negative thoughts, you only undermine your own success.

We play right into **imposter syndrome**, where we feel we aren't good enough, none of our achievements are due to our skills and hard work, and because of this, we'll eventually be exposed as frauds. We tell ourselves it's all luck, or that we've somehow fooled people into thinking we're worthy.

It doesn't matter what you aim to do, whether it's returning to school to start a new career or taking the lead in a meeting. Imposter syndrome is an internal voice that tells you that you have no business calling yourself a programmer, manager, accountant, or grad student. Everyone is smarter than you, and it's only a matter of time before you fail miserably and they see you for the incompetent person you are.

The loudest people sound like they know what they're talking about, but it's often a front to sell themselves.

How to Answer Back

That voice in your head that tells you you're lazy, you're failing, everyone else has it together, is going to be there. I wish I could tell you how to make it stop, but it doesn't.

What I've learned is to talk back to it, at least sometimes.

When it tells me I'm lazy, I remind myself that I have executive dysfunction, a neurological condition. My brain works differently, and struggling with tasks because of how it's wired has nothing to do with choosing not to try.

When it tells me I should be further along by now, I ask myself what I'm measuring against. Nobody starting from a different place is a fair comparison.

When it tells me everyone else can do this easily, I remember I'm looking at their highlight reel. I see all my struggles, failures, and mistakes. They're hiding theirs like I hide mine.

When it tells me I accomplished nothing today, I count what I did. I got out of bed, ate breakfast, and did three things on my **Task List**, which are three I wasn't able to do in the past. On my worst days, getting out of bed was an accomplishment.

When it tells me I'm a failure, I remember that I'm still here and still trying, which means I haven't given up.

The voice knows which insecurities to use against me because it sounds like me and has access to everything I've ever been afraid of or ashamed of. There are days I can recognize what it's doing and shut it up. There are other days it wins, and I believe every word, accomplish nothing, and feel terrible about myself.

You have that voice telling you the same lies. Learn to question it instead of automatically believing it. Sometimes you'll still believe it anyway, but the more you question it, the more you'll notice when it's lying, and the less power it has over what you do next.

The Task List can't help you when the problem isn't the tasks. It's what's running in the background while you're trying to do them.

Change the Channel

Negative thoughts drain you and eat into your ability to focus and get anything done. As someone with a memory that retains everything, I know how hard it is to let these thoughts go. We have so many thoughts entering our minds that it's easy to get sidetracked ruminating on bad memories, obsessing over what may happen in our current life, or dealing with intrusive thoughts nobody wants.

What if we did the opposite of the negative thinking we're prone to do? Instead, we expect our day to be fantastic. Yes, bad things could happen. If they happen, they happen. We address it only when and if it occurs. Then, we don't have to live with the constant anxiety of waiting for it to ambush us, like waiting for that email from your boss telling you you're fired. We spend far too much energy imagining things within the realm of possibility that are entirely unrealistic.

When these ruminating thoughts come in, close your eyes, take a deep breath, and repeat, “Not now. Not today.” Just four words. You can change those thoughts. Switch your thinking to whatever topics interest you at the moment. Bring your thoughts out of past and the future and back into the present.

If you're sure it's hopeless, that it'll all crash and burn, you stop trying, and that's exactly what will happen.

You have more control over your thoughts than it feels like. You can't always stop them from appearing, but you can control how much attention you give them. The second you recognize a negative thought, shut it down. If you can brush it off right away and give it less of your energy, it's less likely to return over time.

When it pops back into your head, tell yourself you already let it go. Imagine breaking a tiny bottle of champagne over it, wishing it bon voyage, or better yet, “I hope I never see you again,” and watching it sail off into the sunset. If there was a lesson to learn from this memory, you've learned it, and now you've moved on.

Then, remind yourself that this is now a phantom thought that doesn't exist.

That may sound ridiculous, but it helps. It takes practice, but you'll get better at it.

I'm not going to tell you to do a two-week meditation retreat in Northern California and align your chakras while sitting in a circle with total strangers. But a few minutes to clear your head when the overwhelm is building can bring the stress down a notch or two.

If you can't dismiss the negative thought immediately, ask yourself why it's happening. Be aware of how you're feeling. Are you nervous? Sad? Anxious? Scared? Lonely?

Repeat that this is not the time to think about this. It's done and in the past. You've learned the lesson. Or, if it's a future worry, you'll think about it only when and if the time comes that you need to confront it.

Change your physical environment. Do something different. Go to a different room, to a different location entirely, or outside, if possible.

Think about something positive that you're interested in. This is one time when letting yourself get drawn into an anti-task is the right call. A negative spiral you can't get out of is worse than not getting your task done.

Do an activity that requires your full attention. Call a friend, play a challenging game, or go for a bike ride.

Don't let upsetting memories from yesterday or unlikely possibilities for tomorrow steal your today.

Give Yourself Credit

Do you give yourself the same amount of praise as you do criticism when you make a mistake? The answer is almost certainly no.

You've done all your grocery shopping and are standing in line with a full cart at the cash register when you realize you forgot your phone so you can't pay. Is your first thought, "You idiot, how could you forget your phone?" For most of us, it is. We don't even consider the circumstances that caused the error.

We don't give ourselves the same praise when we do what we're supposed to do correctly. You never say to yourself, "You remembered everything you needed for work every day this week, your keys, phone, lunch, and laptop bag. Great job, you amazing person." Who would ever say that, right? But it's true. Chances are, you don't give yourself credit for what you do right. You only tear yourself down when things go wrong.

We downplay our achievements but blow our errors out of proportion.

We often take it one step further and scrutinize our actions, intentionally looking for things to criticize. We reflect on our interactions with people and dissect every word, look, and action to find fault in what we've done. It's almost as if we look for reasons to justify our poor self-image.

The self-praise-to-self-criticism ratio is disproportionate because we expect ourselves to be perfect 100% of the time. We can be harsh on ourselves when we fall short of that expectation.

We make far more decisions than we realize each day, most of them without conscious thought, and we get the overwhelming majority of them right. The errors are a tiny fraction of the total. Yet we let that minuscule number of errors dominate our moods and emotions.

Give yourself credit on the days that do go well. It costs you nothing, and you've earned it.

In my senior year of high school, our teachers led us through a practice graduation ceremony two weeks before the actual ceremony. One of the things they instructed us on was how to shake hands with the principal to accept our diplomas.

Shake with the right hand and take the diploma with the left. Seemed simple enough.

But, like a typical neurodivergent kid, I obsessed over this. I was not the type who wanted the slightest bit of public attention. As awkward as I was, I pleaded to skip the ceremony altogether, but my mom insisted that was off the table. I knew I'd be overwhelmed walking across the stage in clothes that didn't feel right and in new shoes I'd never worn before, with thousands of eyes tracking my every move across what seemed like a half-mile stage, and I'd inevitably blow it.

I practiced my handshake for weeks. It had to become second nature.

I had constant back-and-forth conversations with myself. "Don't screw it up." Followed by, "You'll screw it up. You know you will."

During the ceremony, I nervously kept track of how my classmates were faring until my name was called. Not one fumble so far. While the other students enjoyed the afternoon, celebrating four years of hard work and our entrance into adulthood, I was focused only on doing this one thing right.

So, when my name was read, I lumbered across the stage, carefully taking each step. I shook with my right hand. So far, so good. Then...I grabbed my diploma with the same hand.

Luckily, school was out for the summer, so I didn't have to face my classmates beyond that day.

And here I am, still telling the story decades later. It didn't leave me. But now I've come to terms with it. It doesn't cause me to have sleepless nights like it once did. I learned the lesson and (mostly) let it go.

I never believed that I'd do it correctly. I was so in my head with doubt that I choked and failed. Whether it was memorable to anyone else in the auditorium is another question. I'm probably the only one who thought about it beyond the initial moment, though hundreds of people in the packed gym witnessed it and, to my horror, some possibly recorded it.

If the same thing happened to a friend, I'd tell them it doesn't matter, and not one person in that auditorium would care. But, in my irrational thinking, it was different for me. I couldn't get this one thing right, and I felt terrible not only because I failed at it but because I so publicly failed.

That internal voice is relentless, but it's not the only thing that's fighting you. There's also external pressure, the hustle culture, the comparison game, and the constant feeling that you're falling behind.

Stop Playing the Hustle Game

The hustle bros give you the same cookie-cutter advice with the same tired mantras repeated ad nauseam. "Wake up at 4 a.m. Hit the gym. Never stop. Always hustle. Win." That's simple to say but impossible to put into practice because we're human. Of course, if we could work around the clock seven days a week, we might be stratospherically productive, but sadly, we'd also be dead not too long after. It's not feasible as the mortal entities we are.

That's also where a lot of the comparison comes from. The standard you're measuring yourself against isn't the person next to you. There's an entire machine built on the idea that if you're not producing at max capacity at all times, you're falling behind. The people running at that pace are either burning out, faking it, or doing damage to themselves that won't be visible for years.

Their rules are fixed. Yours don't have to be. When your strategies stop working, let them change. You're not the same person from age 20 to 30 or 40 to 50. Your likes and dislikes will fluctuate. You may get burned out on something only to return to it a decade later. Realign your goals to where you are today and keep going. It's expected that you don't get it right the first time or the third. Many successful people changed careers entirely well into their working lives.

I'll never be at the level that the hustle bros demand, but for me, that grind is a guaranteed ticket to burnout.

I get more done now than I ever did by following their advice. It may not be 10 hours or even four hours a day on some days, but it's changed everything.

The Days You Can't Control

Sometimes a deadline won't help us. When circumstances are out of our control, when we travel, when we're thrown into an unfamiliar environment, or when there's a change in our household situation, keeping our emotions in check becomes more difficult. Even tasks we feel are everyday staples can become exponentially more challenging.

The imbalance is evident in our declining productivity, and when this happens, it's easy to get thrown into a negative spiral that's hard to escape. We often blame ourselves for it. Instead, we should recognize that we're out of our element and accept that our situation is demanding more of us than we can give.

And there will always be one more thing you should be doing on top of all of that.

Today, I may be unable to do what I'm supposed to, and everything won't always go as planned. There's a freedom in not being scheduled that rigidly scheduled people never get to experience. Sometimes there's adventure in living in the moment. You may intend to follow through with what you need to do, but you're still learning and growing if it goes a different way.

Consider the things you do every day in normal circumstances. You're ahead of the game if you can complete them, even if you don't do them in the usual time or order.

What if You Fail?

What's done is done. You can't change it now. You may have had great success in your life, or you may feel like nothing significant has happened yet.

It doesn't matter now. You can always start from here. What we think of as past "failures" aren't always actual failures. That depends on how we view them.

We're quick to place blame on ourselves when our decisions don't work out, but don't beat yourself up for past decisions. You didn't have the luxury of knowing all the facts you know now.

Whatever mistakes we made, we can look at what went wrong, make the corrections, and move on.

Sometimes we fail because of our own actions, and sometimes it's because of things we can't control. You're only a true failure when you take nothing away from the experience and continue repeating the same patterns.

If you try something new and it doesn't work, you still know more than you did before.

Almost everything we do can be corrected to some degree. If we can't undo an action entirely, we can at least try to minimize the damage. In the long run, learning from mistakes can be more valuable than doing it right the first time.

You started further back than most of the people you compare yourself to, and every step is harder. That's not fair, and it's not your fault. But you're still here trying, which means you've already done more than they'll ever have to. That voice will tell you it doesn't matter. It's wrong.

Those are the **Ghost Habits**. But there's one more thing.

Conclusion

You Were Never the Problem

Don't overcomplicate it. You don't need elaborate planners, complex schedules, or expensive tools. You need the eight **Ghost Habits** and the willingness to adapt them to your life.

If you take one concept from this book, make it this. The Ghost Habits aren't one-size-fits-all. Use the ones that fit and ignore the rest.

You know what you want to do. You know what helps you. You've read 13 chapters encouraging you to trust that knowledge, so trust it.

Accommodate your neurodivergence. Use your strengths and work around what gets in your way.

What you want for your life and how to get there with the least planning, frustration, and wasted energy are the only questions worth asking.

We take it personally when life doesn't work out the way we want. But we're not giving ourselves the credit we deserve when we view it this way.

When two people meet and try to make a go of a romantic relationship, and it doesn't work out, we don't label them as defective. We say their personalities aren't suited to each other.

When someone lands a new job and doesn't work well with their boss or within their role in the organization, we don't label them as incompetent. We say they're not a good fit for the position or that particular management style.

In both examples, people would say they're just incompatible, and that's OK.

So why do we say neurodivergent people are inferior in some way? We take it to heart because we think it's our fault. We think we're actively undermining our situation, or we're too stupid to learn what everyone else already knows.

However, the reality is that many of us are simply incompatible with society in terms of our work abilities. And in turn, as is the main theme of this book, we are incompatible with the standard advice given to fix that problem.

Our functioning styles don't mesh with how the world is set up, so we find our own way to do things.

When Every Day Is a Struggle

Maybe you came from a difficult background. Maybe you're dealing with circumstances that make every single day harder than it needs to be. Poverty, chronic illness, trauma, systemic barriers that were never your fault, but you're stuck dealing with anyway.

You're still the only one who can change where you go from here. No one else is going to do the work for you. You can get help along the way. Therapy, medication, support groups, use whatever resources you can find.

You're the one who has to pick up the sheet of paper and write down those three tasks. You don't know what you don't know. If what you're doing isn't working, the answer might be something you haven't discovered yet.

Depending on where you are in life, your first step may feel as easy as getting up off the couch or as enormous as crossing the Grand Canyon on a tightrope. Either way, the first step is the same. If none of the Ghost Habits feel possible right now, start with the Six Survival Steps.

When everything lines up, this is what it looks like for me. My best days are when I wake up after a good eight hours of sleep.

I fill up my coffee cup, check the socials, and get some writing done. Before long, I'm thinking about what I can do next, whether it's cleaning the car, making appointments I haven't been in the mood to make, or getting back to people I've put off replying to for much too long. Those are the days when everything comes together, and I get something or many things done.

I don't set out to make those days happen. I can't control it. But I know what they feel like when I'm in them.

This is yours, not the productivity gurus', not the hustle bros'. You've spent too long trying to fit yourself into systems designed for people who don't think, struggle, or experience the world as you do. The eight Ghost Habits are tools. Use them when they help. Ignore them when they don't. Adapt them to fit your life.

One Last Thing About Habits

I spent this entire book giving you tools.

That doesn't mean habits are bad or wrong. It means they're optional.

Some people build habits and routines that work well. Some people can't maintain them no matter how hard they try. And some don't want to bother.

If you have a morning routine that helps, keep it. If habit tracking motivates you, use it. If you've built systems that work for your brain, keep using them.

The eight Ghost Habits aren't meant to replace what's working. They're a different approach for people who either can't maintain traditional habits or don't want to try.

Habits work for some people. They don't work for others. This book is the without them option.

Use what works. Ghost what doesn't.

What To Do When

"I can't pick which task to do"

Use the Task of Least Resistance from your Task List. Pick the easiest thing on your list and do that one. Ghost Habit #4.

"I keep switching between tasks and finishing nothing"

Pick one task, the Task of Least Resistance, and stay on it until you finish or you truly can't focus anymore. Don't let yourself jump to the next thing. Ghost Habit #4.

"I started using the Task List and now I've stopped"

You crashed. That happens to everyone using these tools. Go to Ghost Habit #2 and use the Restart Rule.

"The Task List isn't working"

Are you not using it, or is it not helping? If you stopped using it, come back when you're ready. If it's not helping, you may be putting too much in the Now box. Ghost Habit #4.

"I can't stop doing the anti-task"

You're depleted and need real rest. Nap. Go outside. Do nothing. If you have deadlines, use the Hard Start Principle. Ghost Habit #5.

"I don't have any motivation at all"

For tasks with consequences, you don't need motivation. The deadline does the work. For everything else, wait for the Ready Window. Ghost Habit #5. If you have no motivation for anything at all, you might be depressed or burned out. Talk to someone.

"I keep crashing"

Occasional crashes are expected. Use the Restart Rule.

If it's frequent, you're pushing too hard. Ghost Habit #7. If it's constant, something in your life needs to change. Ghost Habit #6.

"The Hard Start Principle isn't working"

Does the task actually have to be done right now? If not, do it later. If yes, make it smaller. Not the whole task, just the first physical movement. If you still can't move, call someone. Ghost Habit #5.

"I feel guilty about resting"

That's the productivity culture talking. Rest is for survival, not a reward. If you don't rest, you'll crash harder later. Ghost Habit #8.

"I want to use habits instead"

Then use them. This book is for people who've tried habits and can't maintain them. If you can build habits and they work for you, keep doing that. The Ghost Habits are an alternative, not a replacement for what's already working.

Glossary

These are the terms used throughout the book.

ADHD inertia

The neurological tendency to stay stuck in whatever state you're already in. If you're doing nothing, starting is hard. If you're working, stopping is hard. It's also what makes it difficult to build habits and to interrupt hyperfocus. The Ghost Habits are designed to work around it rather than fight it.

Anti-tasks

What you do instead of what you're supposed to do. Anti-tasks aren't random distractions. They're your brain's solution to a problem with your current task. They provide dopamine, rest, escape, novelty, or social connection that your real task isn't providing. Anti-tasks are information about what you need.

Anticipation paralysis

A type of paralysis that happens before you even start a task. You're dreading the task so much that you can't make yourself begin. The starting is the hard part, not the doing. You'll do anything else, including tasks you normally hate, to avoid starting the thing you're supposed to do.

Biphasic sleep
A sleep pattern where you sleep in two separate periods rather than one continuous block. Typically, a longer night's sleep and a shorter nap during the day. More common in neurodivergent people than generally recognized.

Body doubling
Working in the presence of another person, in the same room or virtually, to help you stay on task. The other person doesn't have to be doing the same work or even interacting with you. Their presence alone is often enough to reduce the pull of anti-tasks and help you stay focused.

Consequence
The result of not doing something. Immediate consequences (such as getting fired, being evicted, or failing a class) motivate action. Distant or vague consequences (health problems decades away, personal disappointment) don't motivate action for most people. Tasks with real, immediate consequences get done. Tasks without them don't.

Crash

When you stop functioning and can't do anything productive. It happens to everyone who uses these tools, and it's expected. Rest. Come back when you're ready.

Decision paralysis

When you have too many options, your brain locks up trying to choose. You need to pick one thing to work on, but you've got 25 things on your list. So you don't start at all, or you switch between tasks every five minutes and finish nothing. Solution: Task of Least Resistance.

Demand paralysis

When someone else puts a time limit on you and your brain shuts down. The urgency that's supposed to help you start is the same thing stopping you.

Doable deadline

An upcoming event you're looking forward to that still creates waiting paralysis. A concert, lunch with a friend, or picking up your kid from school. Positive anticipation causes the same stuck, can't-do-anything paralysis as dread does. The event doesn't have to be bad to shut your brain down.

Doom deadline

An external deadline with real consequences you didn't choose. Work projects, bill due dates, and appointments you can't miss. The consequences of missing them are severe enough to override the paralysis.

Doomscrolling

Compulsively scrolling through social media or news, usually negative content, past the point of any benefit. A common rest-seeking or escape-seeking anti-task. It feels like rest, but leaves you more depleted than when you started.

Dopamine

A chemical neurotransmitter in your brain that signals potential reward and pleasure. Your brain constantly seeks dopamine, which is why you can focus for hours on video games but can't reply to one text message.

Eisenhower Matrix

A productivity tool that sorts tasks into four categories based on urgency and importance. Do it now, schedule it, delegate it, or eliminate it. The Ghost Habits Task List uses a similar four-box structure, organized around what you can do right now rather than what's most important.

Executive dysfunction

Difficulty with planning, organizing, starting tasks, switching between tasks, and following through. Executive dysfunction is a neurological condition, not laziness or lack of motivation. It's common in people with ADHD, autism, depression, anxiety, and other conditions. The Ghost Habits tools are designed to work with executive dysfunction rather than fight it.

Ghost Habits

Tools that appear when you need them and disappear when you don't. No streaks, no failure when you stop. When you're ready to come back, you start the same way you started the first time.

Hard Start Principle

For when a task has to get done and nothing else is working. Not for total paralysis. Use the Six Survival Steps for that. For when you're stuck on a task your brain is refusing. Three questions: Does it have to be done now? What can your hands do right now? Who am I doing this for?

Hyperfixation

An intense, consuming focus on a particular interest or activity that can completely take over your time and attention. Different from hyperfocus, which is about a task. Common in neurodivergent people.

Hyperfocus

Intense concentration on one task where you lose track of time and can't stop even when you need to.

Hyperfocus can produce a lot of work, but it often damages your health and leads to crashes. Different from superfocus.

Hyperfocus Crash

What happens after an extended hyperfocus session. You've been running at full capacity for hours or days, only to stop functioning. The crash is proportional to how hard you pushed. Rest is the only way through it.

Imposter syndrome

The internal voice that tells you your achievements aren't real, your skills aren't enough, and it's only a matter of time before everyone finds out you don't belong. You feel like a fraud even when the evidence says otherwise. Common in neurodivergent people who've spent years being told they're not capable.

Junebugging

A method for getting through household tasks or similar work when your brain won't stay on one thing, originating in the ADHD community around 2020. Pick a location or task as your home base and always return to it, no matter what else you get pulled into along the way. You empty the trash, notice the floor needs sweeping, sweep it, then return to the bathroom you were cleaning. You keep returning until the home base task is done.

Known task paralysis

When your brain refuses a task you've done before and already knows everything about. You have the full picture before you start, and that's enough to stop you.

Masking

Suppressing or hiding neurodivergent traits to appear neurotypical in social or professional situations. Forcing eye contact, suppressing stims, following social scripts that don't come naturally, and staying quiet about being overwhelmed. Masking takes significant energy and the cost accumulates. By the time you get home after a day of masking, the energy that was supposed to go toward your own life is already gone.

NEET

Not in Employment, Education, or Training. A term used to describe people who are not working, studying, or in any formal training program. Common in neurodivergent adults who struggle with traditional employment or education structures.

Neurodivergent

A brain that works differently from what's considered typical or "normal." Includes ADHD, autism, dyslexia, and other conditions that affect how you think, learn, and process information. Traditional productivity advice is designed for neurotypical brains and often doesn't work for neurodivergent people.

Neurotypical

A brain that works in ways considered typical or "normal" by society. Most productivity advice is created for neurotypical brains and assumes habits, routines, and discipline work reliably.

Overwhelm paralysis

When a task feels too big, and you don't know where to start, you don't. Your brain sees the enormity of what needs to be done and shuts down. You can't even break it into smaller pieces because that feels like too much work. Solution: Do the smallest possible thing related to the task.

Perfectionism paralysis

When you're frozen because you're terrified of doing something wrong. If you can't do it perfectly, you won't do it at all. So the project sits there, haunting you as you research and prepare, but you never start. Perfectionism paralysis stops more projects than actual failure does.

Pomodoro Technique

A time management method that divides work into timed intervals, usually 25 minutes, followed by short breaks. Popular productivity advice recommends it. For many neurodivergent people, it doesn't work because the timer interrupts hyperfocus at the worst moment, and the artificial structure creates more anxiety than it relieves.

Productive bouncing

When your brain refuses to stay on one task, switching between multiple real tasks and making actual progress on each one. Different from procrastination bouncing, where you're staying busy but avoiding the thing that needs doing. Productive bouncing isn't efficient, but it works when your brain won't cooperate any other way.

Ready Window

For tasks without deadlines or consequences, wait until you're thinking about the task and feel like doing it. Then do it immediately. Don't wait for a better time. That moment of natural motivation might not come back.

Restart Rule

What to do when a goal or project fails. Regroup by asking whether you wanted it and what got in the way. Refocus by figuring out where it went wrong and how you'd approach it differently. Return by trying again with what you've learned.

Six Survival Steps

What to do when you're completely paralyzed and can't do anything. For when your brain has completely checked out. Starts with a survival check, then builds momentum with the smallest possible actions.

Stimming

Self-stimulatory behavior. Repetitive physical movements or sounds that help regulate emotions, reduce anxiety, or manage sensory overload. Rocking, tapping, pacing, humming, fidgeting. Stimming is a natural neurological response, not a behavior to be eliminated. Suppressing it takes energy and is part of masking.

Superfocus

When you're fully engaged with your work. Time passes quickly, but you can leave the task if something important comes up. You're aware of your body and can stop when you need to. Different from hyperfocus because you're in control.

Task List

One sheet of paper divided into four boxes: Now, Later, Everyday, Remember. Your organizational tool. What you're working on right now.

Task of Least Resistance

When you can't decide which task to do, pick the one that requires the least mental effort right now. Don't think about importance or urgency. Pick the easiest one and do it. This gets you started, which makes the next task easier.

Time bite

A small chunk of wasted time between appointments or obligations. 20 minutes before you have to leave for an appointment. 10 minutes while waiting in line. Time bites are too short for deep work but long enough to do something small.

Time blindness

Difficulty perceiving how much time has passed or accurately estimating how long a task will take. Common in neurodivergent people. You sit down to work for twenty minutes, and two hours disappear. Or you're certain you have enough time, only to be suddenly late. Time blindness is neurological, not carelessness.

Notes on Research

This book draws on peer-reviewed research about ADHD, autism, executive dysfunction, and dopamine systems. Rather than interrupt the flow with citations throughout, the references are gathered at the end of the book in the Notes section for readers who want to explore further.

The strategies are grounded in that research and informed by years of living with executive dysfunction myself. Where the research ends, experience fills in.

I'm not a therapist, psychologist, or medical doctor. Many books about neurodivergence and executive dysfunction are written by researchers. This one is written by someone who lives it.

Notes

Introduction

“There’s a name for it, ADHD inertia, and it works exactly like it sounds.”: Barkley, R. A. (2015). *Attention-deficit hyperactivity disorder: A handbook for diagnosis and treatment* (4th ed.). Guilford Press.

The Struggle Is Real

“20% of the global population have at least one neurodivergent condition.”: Doyle, N. (2020). Neurodiversity at work: A biopsychosocial model and the impact on working adults. *British Medical Bulletin*, 135(1), 108–125.

“Unemployment among neurodivergent adults is significantly higher than the general population, and for adults with autism, the number may reach upwards of 85%.”: Griffiths, A. J., Hanson, A. H., Giannantonio, C. M., Mathur, S. K., Hyde, K., & Linstead, E. (2020). Developing employment environments where individuals with ASD thrive: Using machine learning to explore employer policies and practices. *Brain Sciences*, 10(9), 632. https://doi.org/10.3390/brainsci10090632

Masking and energy depletion.: Cage, E., & Troxell-Whitman, Z. (2019). Understanding the reasons, contexts and costs of camouflaging for autistic adults. *Journal of Autism and Developmental Disorders*, 49(5), 1899–1911. https://doi.org/10.1007/s10803-018-03878-x

Why You Can't Get Started (And Why That's Not Your Fault)

Dopamine and executive dysfunction claims.: Barkley, R. A. (2015). *Attention-deficit hyperactivity disorder: A handbook for diagnosis and treatment* (4th ed.). Guilford Press.

Dopamine seeking and reward deficiency in ADHD.: Volkow, N. D., Wang, G. J., Kollins, S. H., Wigal, T. L., Newcorn, J. H., Telang, F., Fowler, J. S., Zhu, W., Logan, J., Ma, Y., Pradhan, K., Wong, C., & Swanson, J. M. (2009). Evaluating dopamine reward pathway in ADHD: Clinical implications. JAMA, 302(10), 1084–1091. https://doi.org/10.1001/jama.2009.1308

Diamond, A. (2013). Executive functions. *Annual Review of Psychology*, 64, 135–168. https://doi.org/10.1146/annurev-psych-113011-143750

The six paralysis types described in this chapter are the author's framework synthesizing established research on executive dysfunction, procrastination, and perfectionism. For the underlying research, see: Barkley (2015) above; Steinert, Heim & Leichsenring (2021) for perfectionism and anticipation paralysis; and Oroian, Nechita & Szalontay (2025) for decision paralysis specifically.

Oroian, B. A., Nechita, P., & Szalontay, A. (2025). ADHD and decision paralysis: Overwhelm in a world of choices. *European Psychiatry*, 68(S1), S161. https://doi.org/10.1192/j.eurpsy.2025.406

Steinert, C., Heim, N., & Leichsenring, F. (2021). Procrastination, perfectionism, and other work-related mental problems: Prevalence, types, assessment, and treatment — a scoping review. *Frontiers in Psychiatry*, 12, 736776. https://doi.org/10.3389/fpsyt.2021.736776

You Don't Need Habits

Pomodoro Technique.: Cirillo, F. (2006). The Pomodoro Technique. FC Garage.

Time blindness.: Barkley, R. A. (2015). *Attention-deficit hyperactivity disorder: A handbook for diagnosis and treatment* (4th ed.). Guilford Press.

Don't Plan to Plan

Neurodivergent associative thinking and divergent creativity.: Stolte, M., Trindade-Pons, V., Vlaming, P., Jakobi, B., Franke, B., Kroesbergen, E. H., Baas, M., & Hoogman, M. (2022). Characterizing creative thinking and creative achievements in relation to symptoms of attention-deficit/hyperactivity disorder and autism spectrum disorder. *Frontiers in Psychiatry*, 13, 909202. https://doi.org/10.3389/fpsyt.2022.909202

Body doubling.: Eagle, T., Baltaxe-Admony, L. B., & Ringland, K. E. (2024). "It was something I naturally found worked and heard about later": An investigation of body doubling with neurodivergent participants. ACM *Transactions on Accessible Computing*, 17(3), Article 16. https://doi.org/10.1145/3689648

Do What You Can When You Can

Junebugging: The term originated in ADHD online communities (c. 2020) and spread primarily through Reddit and TikTok. There is no single primary source. The method is community-developed and the name derives from the June bug beetle's behavior of returning repeatedly to the same location.

Create Your Workspace

"For people with ADHD, sleep disturbances affect around 60%.": van der Ham, M., Bijlenga, D., Böhmer, M., Beekman, A. T. F., & Kooij, S. (2024). Sleep problems in adults with ADHD: Prevalences and their relationship with psychiatric comorbidity. *Journal of Attention Disorders*, 28(13), 1642–1652. https://doi.org/10.1177/10870547241284477

Sleep duration recommendations.: Hirshkowitz, M., Whiton, K., Albert, S. M., et al. (2015). National Sleep Foundation's sleep time duration recommendations: Methodology and results summary. *Sleep Health*, 1(1), 40–43. https://doi.org/10.1016/j.sleh.2015.10.004

Walking and prolonged sitting.: Duran, A. T., Friel, C. P., Serafini, M. A., Ensari, I., Cheung, Y. K., & Diaz, K. M. (2023). Breaking up prolonged sitting to improve cardiometabolic risk: Dose-response analysis of a randomized crossover trial. *Medicine & Science in Sports & Exercise*, 55(5), 847-855. https://doi.org/10.1249/MSS.0000000000003109

Stay in the Zone (Then Get Out)

Hyperfocus.: Ashinoff, B. K., & Abu-Akel, A. (2021). Hyperfocus: The forgotten frontier of attention. *Psychological Research*, 85(1), 1–19. https://doi.org/10.1007/s00426-019-01245-8

Take the Downtime You Need

Cumulative exhaustion and neurodivergent burnout.: Raymaker, D. M., Teo, A. R., Steckler, N. A., Lentz, B., Scharer, M., Delos Santos, A., Kapp, S. K., Hunter, M., Joyce, A., & Nicolaidis, C. (2020). "Having all of your internal resources exhausted beyond measure and being left with no clean-up crew": Defining autistic burnout. *Autism in Adulthood*, 2(2), 132–143. https://doi.org/10.1089/aut.2019.0079

Resources

Finding the right support depends on where you live and what you need. For a list of resources, including mental health support, diagnosis pathways, and helplines by country, visit resources.ghosthabits.com.

If you are in the US and need emergency mental health support, call or text 988.

Did This Book Help?

If Ghost Habits helped you, here's how you can help other people find it.

Leave a review on Amazon, Apple Books, Kobo, or wherever you bought it. If you use Goodreads or StoryGraph, a review there helps too. Reviews help other neurodivergent people find a book that was written for them.

Share one thing that worked for you on social media. Tag it #GhostHabits so others can find it.

Send the Six Survival Steps to someone who's stuck. Point them to ghosthabits.com where they can download them free.

Tell one person who struggles with traditional productivity advice. Sometimes the best recommendation comes from someone else who gets it.

About the Author

N.D. Olson got the idea for Ghost Habits years ago and never got around to writing it. Which, given what the book is about, makes perfect sense.

It was written on endless espressos and a coffeehouse-sounds playlist, between day hikes, tending a stubborn urban garden, and too much reality TV and true crime podcasts. The cat sat in on every session but was entirely unhelpful.

Find N.D. Olson at ghosthabits.com.

www.ingramcontent.com/pod-product-compliance
Lightning Source LLC
Chambersburg PA
CBHW031341230926
51848CB00002B/331
* 9 7 8 9 1 9 8 9 0 9 9 0 6 *